CASH FLOW SECRET$

Real Estate, Investing &
Wealth Management Principles...
They Failed To Teach You In School

W. J. MANDRELL, III

Show Us
Your New Book!

Share a photo of yourself wherever you're reading this book today!

Insta @wjmandrell

FB /wmandrell

#CashFlowSecrets

#RealWeathBooks

Author Limit of Liability: Please note that much of this publication is based on personal experience and anecdotal evidence. Although the author and publisher have made every reasonable attempt to achieve complete accuracy of the content of this book, they make no warranties with respect to the accuracy or completeness of the contents of this book in specific disclaim any implied warranties of any merchantability or fitness for particular purpose. Your particular circumstances may not be suited to the examples illustrated in this book; in fact, they likely will not be. You should use the information in this book at your own risk. Nothing in this book is intended to replace common sense or legal, accounting, or professional advice, and it is meant only to inform.

Real Wealth Books

FIRST EDITION

www.RealWealthBooks.com

Real Wealth Books, LLC
288 Grove St Suite, Suite 337
Braintree, MA. 02184

Praise for Cash Flow Secrets

"Thank you for everything that you do and the work that you put in to reach new heights. Your work ethic, knowledge, and the way you choose to give back certainly do not go unnoticed. I look forward to continuing to follow your journey!"

- A. Abad | Boston, MA

"Willie is the most humble, knowledgeable, honest real estate investor I've come across. He shares wisdom you can implement on day one and his strategies to BUILD WEALTH are tried, tested and proven. If you want to build your rental portfolio... this book is a must read."

- D. McDonald | Orlando, FL

"Willie's leadership and expertise are unparalleled in the real estate world and he's constantly learning, lending a helping hand, and advocating for others who are looking to build wealth in this industry."

- J. Thomas | Springfield, MA

"All of Willie's know-how compiled in this book will definitely provide an advantage to any investor in making wise wealth-building decisions."

- R. Moise | Atlanta, GA

"*Cash Flow Secrets* demonstrates that being successful in the real estate industry is not about luck, but the knowledge you acquire and how effectively you use that knowledge. I highly recommend anyone looking to get into real estate to learn from Willie."

- L. Boatwright | Baton Rouge, LA

Dedicated to the Ladies:

To my wife, for always believing in me and encouraging me, no matter how crazy my dreams have been.

To my mother, for being the strong woman that you are and helping my brothers and I get through rough times. For teaching me how to overcome adversity and helping me become the man I am today.

To my grandmother, for introducing me to the real estate game. For helping me lay down the foundation and shining a light on the path to wealth. Rest in peace.

I hope each of you are proud.

Table of Contents

Introduction:

My grandmother, Josephine Barren, moved to Boston from Macon, Georgia in the 1950s. At the time, she had a sixth-grade education and very little money in her pocket. She was determined to get away from the South and the slow lifestyle of work on the family farm. When she arrived in Boston, she waited tables, worked on textile manufacturing lines, and served drinks at a few different nightclubs.

Her life took an unexpected turn when a mentor suggested she invest in a boarding house in the South End of Boston. In the late 1950's, the South End was rundown and impoverished, a completely different neighborhood than it is today. Not too many people wanted to invest in the neighborhood, so my grandmother was able to buy a brownstone for around $50,000. She lived in one room and rented out the others, paying off the mortgage and various property expenses each month. It was during this time that she met and married my grandfather, Willie James Mandrell Senior, an active Army sergeant. In 1963, they adopted my father, Willie James Mandrell Junior, and my uncle, Frank Mandrell, a couple years after that.

By the mid-1960s, the South End was starting to change. The 52-story Prudential Center was built 2 blocks away and sparked a tremendous amount of economic growth in the area. My grandparents were in the direct path of progress. As their property values increased, so did their brownstone's rent, which in turn, gave them access to additional loans.

From there they decided to buy 2 more brownstones in this neighborhood that they loved. The goal was simply to repeat the process and create multiple streams of income for themselves. There was no direct deposit, no fancy accounting software, no computers, no email, no cell phones. They kept things simple. They collected rent every month, paid off the bills every month, and kept what was left over for themselves.

I think as a result, my father was given a lot of things in life. He lived in a nice home in a nice neighborhood, was driven around in a nice car, and wore the best clothes. He was a tap dancer, played on the football team, and my grandparents entered both him and my uncle into various local talent shows. My father and uncle also appeared on several TV game shows.

My mother's childhood differed greatly from my father's. They lived in the same city, but at opposite ends of the wealth spectrum. Her basic needs were met, but not much more than that. My mother and father met at Cathedral High School, fell in love, and had me a few years after their graduation in 1983. My grandmother continued to hand things to my father, including a 6-bedroom house as an investment and payment for his college education at Northeastern University. Within a couple of years, he had unsurprisingly dropped out, lost the property, and started using drugs. In 1988, when I was 5 years old, my grandfather passed away. My father walked out on his family around this time, and I didn't see or hear from him again for the next 27 years.

My mother and grandmother never really saw things eye-to-eye. The loss of my grandfather and the disappearance of my father drove a deeper wedge into their relationship and prompted my mother to set off on her own with me and my siblings in tow. Over the next decade, we spent time in various shelters and public housing facilities in the Greater Boston area. My brothers and I bounced through 5 or 6 different school systems because my mother failed to stay settled for long. We spent 10 months out of the year struggling, but for 2 dream-filled months every summer, my mother allowed us to stay with Grandma Josephine. Once there, we were treated like young princes. During this 10-year span, my grandmother also started to sell off her real estate portfolio. She was getting older, and the physical aspects of property management were starting to take a toll on her without the help of her husband or children. She sold off her final piece of property, her primary residence for over 40 years, in the summer of 1999.

When she first purchased that brownstone, it cost her approximately $50,000. She later sold it for roughly $900,000. Since then, the brownstone has been converted into multiple condos, and a single unit sold for $1.7 million this year. In total, this building is now worth almost $7 million. Imagine if my father had stayed sober and stuck around...but that's a conversation for another time.

Toward the end of 1998, I artfully convinced my mother that high school was no longer the right fit for me. The classes were uninteresting, and I didn't feel like I was making the most of my time. I dropped out of high school in 1999 and began working random jobs, including stints at McDonald's, a local furniture store, and a couple area restaurants as a prep cook. This was, of course, after I falsified my age on a few documents to become eligible to work. Despite this hustling spirit, it didn't take me long to realize that trading my time for a low, hourly wage was never going to get me anywhere.

Within 18 months of quitting high school, I had completed my GED (graduate equivalency diploma) and enrolled in business classes at a local community college. While I was starting my first year in college, my same-age friends were preparing for senior year in high school. I continued to work while attending college, still in mostly short-lived jobs, but most notably in a nearby Marriott hotel, an Outback Steakhouse, and finally a Honda dealership. I had initially applied to the car dealership as a lot attendant, but the hiring manager took notice of my professionalism and sales-pitching skills. He gave me the opportunity to work as a sales representative.

I got my first taste of real money at the car dealership. I finally understood what it felt like to be directly rewarded for the hard work I put in. Unlike the hourly jobs that I had been working thus far, if I worked harder and smarter than the rest of the salespeople at the dealership, I would earn more money. I also learned how to sell myself as a representative, build rapport with customers, and quickly compute financial calculations for them. It was there that I fell in love with business finance.

In the years that followed this revelation, I transferred from community college to Northeastern University as a finance major. I worked at Citizens Bank, Bank of America, and a few other financial institutions. I earned all of my financial securities industry licenses, including the series 6, 63, 65, 7, and 24. I also bought my first multi-family house in 2006, at the insistence of my grandmother, of course.

Like how the dealership gave me my first taste of self-employment and independent income, my first multi-family property introduced me to the idea of passive income and an understanding of how real wealth is built. In a sense, I was trying to re-create what my grandmother had built. Over the years, she always reminded me that she was a black woman from the South with a sixth-grade education who had bought real estate in Boston in the 1950's and 60's. "Have you ever known me to work?" She knew the answer was no, at least, not in a traditional sense.

As far back as I could remember, her only job was to keep her properties clean, find new tenants when someone moved out, and collect rent when it was due. She often told me that "the business wasn't hard." If she could do it with all the hurdles of her early life—and with no college education—then so could I. Her goal with my brothers and I was to not make the same mistakes she had made with my father and uncle. She was determined to give us less and teach us more. She was certainly willing to help us financially, but only after we had proven ourselves. By 2006, I had begun to take the first steps in what she believed was the right direction.

But then came the crashes; first the stock market in 2007, and then the housing market close behind in 2008. I was brand-new to the rental business and saw my home's value decrease by 25 percent within the first few years after buying. I was discouraged, to say the least, but I didn't realize until later that it was a gift in disguise.

I was still in financial services at this time, but due to the stock market crash, my company was going to shit. Little Bernie Madoffs were popping up all over the country and forcing us to make some really tough ethical decisions. Long story short, in 2010, unemployment was high, foreclosures were happening all over the place, and I no longer had a strong belief in the financial services industry.

Although home values in the neighborhood had decreased, I never had problems paying my mortgage on the multi-family house. My tenants were paying 60 percent of my entire mortgage and expenses. I also discovered that since no one was buying in that rough economy, the demand for my rentals was up and, therefore, so were the market rent prices. As tenants moved out for various reasons, I would increase the rent. Soon, my mortgage coverage shifted from 60 to nearly 75 percent being paid by my tenants. My grandmother had been right: this business was not hard.

In late 2010, I decided to quit my financial services job and immerse myself in real estate full-time. I obtained my real estate license and worked for several small brokerages. I read everything I could on the subject, and went to every seminar and networking event possible. I eventually established my niche in the small multi-family market in Boston. I knew I could sell anything that I truly believed in, and I deeply believed in the multi-family rental business. The more I helped clients with their sales, purchases, and leases, the more I understood my local market. The more I understood my market, the better I became at recognizing investment opportunities.

From 2011 to 2014, my girlfriend, Bao (now my wife) and I started buying other rental properties in Boston. She believed in my vision and helped me acquire one of the best performing properties we have today. We were buying during a time when some people were still very afraid of the market and couldn't realize that we were in the midst of a major upswing, especially in the Northeast.

In 2014, my grandmother, my greatest mentor, passed away. This was just 3 months before Bao and I were married. I was heartbroken, and also a little angry. That anger arose because I had always felt the need to work hard enough to prove to my grandmother that I would not turn out like my father, that somebody in the family would continue to build on her legacy. There was so much more I wanted to show her and achieve while she was alive. I felt our time was cut short, and I miss her to this day.

Even after her death, Grandma Josephine continued to teach me lessons. She passed without a will, and while searching through her things, we found 3 handwritten wills, all with separate dates spanning 15 years. Immediately, family members started to appear out of nowhere, making claims to what they believed they were due. Right before she passed, my grandmother had been living in 1 of my rentals and therefore had the most contact with me. My family looked to me to take charge over distributing her assets. Word traveled so far and fast that even my father got wind of her death, appearing for the first time in 27 years after vanishing. He came to collect what he could, and then was off again.

Once we had a chance to dig into my grandmother's finances, I was personally blown away. I found that she had roughly $20,000 in cash and about $47,000 in a brokerage account. This wasn't a small amount of money, but it was a far cry below what I (and others) assumed she had. When I dug a little deeper, I discovered that she had had 2 major problems over the years.

Problem 1: A cousin had encouraged her to invest the majority of her real estate sale proceeds into the stock market. Her previous bank statements showed that the crash of 2007 dealt her a serious blow.

Problem 2: Outside of my grandfather's small military pension, she had no additional income. When she sold her final property in 1999, her cash flow vanished. She traded a continuous stream of income for a lump sum of cash. Had she lived a few years longer, she may have run out of money entirely.

I learned some valuable lessons from the chaos that developed after my grandmother's death, lessons about preparing for the future, insurance policies, estate planning, and asset protection. I began to consider portfolio diversification more seriously, and planned multiple streams of income that will continue long after I retire. I also learned that trying to stockpile enough cash for a comfortable retirement is a fool's gold errand. My grandmother's passing taught me that cash flow is the only way to secure a comfortable financial future.

The information that follows is not stuff that I've heard from somebody else. It's not information I've pulled from Investopedia and regurgitated back to you. Everything on these pages comes from my experiences and/or practices that I have undertaken. They are my successes and failures, along with the lessons that I've learned from experiencing them.

After witnessing multiple economic downturns and the COVID-19 crisis and its resulting recession, I realize this information is needed now more than ever.

The goal of this book is to share with you everything I've learned since the crash of 2008 that has put me in a better position to weather this current storm. *Cash Flow Secrets* is a method to simplify the path toward building wealth. The world makes financial education more complex than it needs to be. This book intends to remove most of the complexity and provide ONLY what you need to know to build wealth.

The book is broken up into 5 sections that are further divided into simple wealth-building concepts that I call "secrets". I've also offered additional reading and other resources if you want to go even deeper into each topic. Finally, I conclude each section with a few action steps for you to take. I don't want this book to be something that you read once and let collect dust on your shelf: think of this as a special set of blueprints to help you build a solid foundation. That way, you can weather the storm of any global crisis or loss that comes your way.

My hope is that this book helps you skip over some of the BS and opens your eyes to some of the possibilities in real estate, no matter your starting point. My hope is that it inspires you to start your own business or pushes you to continue building an amazing cash flow portfolio.

Let's get after it!

Section 1

Let's Get Focused

SECRET 1

What You Think About Really Matters

"Whether you think you can, or think you can't... you're right."

– Henry Ford

Throughout my career and life, I have realized that state of mind is a huge deal. In other words, what I visualize—both positive and negative—*matters.*

Let me ask you a question that was asked to me several years ago: if your 10-year-old daughter told you she wanted to be the first person to walk on Mars, what would you say to her? Would you tell her that if she studied hard and focused, she could do anything she wanted in life? Or would you tell her that her dream was extremely unlikely and unachievable? I think most people would encourage their little girl to dream big, and yet, we tend to have limited beliefs when it comes to ourselves and our own abilities. Society believes that adults should stop dreaming and live "realistic" lives. If that's true, then what's realistic?

I hate the idea of living a "realistic" life. The idea that a young black kid out of public housing own an 8-figure real estate portfolio and author a book on financial literacy might sound unrealistic to some. I want you to stop thinking in those terms. Start asking yourself what you really want out of life. Is your dream something you're willing to work for and make sacrifices to go after?

Most poor people think poor thoughts. They think that money is scarce and that they must hold on to everything that they get. Wealthy people understand that there is an unlimited supply of money, and if they make the right moves, they can have as much as they'd like. Wealthy people see opportunities within every problem. Poor people see problems as convenient excuses to not achieve the things they want in life. The first step on your path to wealth is the hardest step: take charge of the way you think.

KEY POINTS

- Visualize your dreams in a positive light.
- Don't accept society's standards for a "realistic" life.
- Find opportunities within every problem.

MONEY SMARTS

An Alcoholic Father Has Two Sons

The 1st Son Struggles Through Life & Eventually Becomes an Alcoholic

The 2nd Son Becomes a Successful Business Owner & Rental Property Investor

Both Were Asked, "Why Have You Become Who You Are?"

Both Responded, "Because My Father Was an Alcoholic."

Life Is All About Our Choices

MONEY SMARTS

Choose Your Company Wisely

If You Hang Out With 4 Broke People,
You Will Be the 5th

If You Hang Out With 4 Intelligent People,
You Will Be the 5th

If You Hang Out 4 Lazy People,
You Will Be the 5th

If You Hang Out With 4 Millionaires,
You Will Be the 5th

SECRET 2

Most People Are Giving You Bad Advice

"Opportunity is missed by most people because it is dressed in overalls and looks like work."

–Thomas Edison

"If everyone was incredible, no one would be."

That line comes from the 2004 Pixar film *The Incredibles*. Let's think about it for a moment. How can we apply that same concept to money and wealth? If everyone was wealthy, no one would be. If everyone was successful, no one would be. If everyone was the winner, no one would be. If you understand this, then why follow mainstream financial advice? It can't possibly be correct for everyone, right?

To become wealthy, you must realize that the vast majority of people are flat-out wrong when it comes to the subject of money and wealth. Wealthy people tend to run opposite to the crowd. They're the people buying when everyone else is racing to sell. They're the people selling when the vast majority are buying everything in sight. They're the people with the steady hand in a shaky economic environment. In short, the wealthy are *The Incredibles*.

It takes a mentally tough individual to not follow suit when they see friends and family members selling stock, or running to the supermarket to buy up all the supplies they can, or taking their cash out of the banks during times of crisis. But you must stay resolute. Simply put, the wealthy tend to be gritty, resourceful, and strong-minded individuals. They are the people looking left, when, financially, everyone only has eyes for what's on the right.

KEY POINTS

- Mainstream financial advice is often counter-productive.
- The truly successful run in the opposite direction to the crowd.
- To be wealthy is to first be mentally tough in the face of instability and fear: to be *incredible.*

SECRET 3

You Need to Play the Long Game

"Investing should be more like watching paint dry or watching grass grow. If you want excitement, take $800 and go to Las Vegas."

–Paul Samuelson

We live in a society of instant gratification. By that, I mean most of us are short-term thinkers. Everyone wants everything today or tomorrow, or it's not worth pursuing. When I say everyone, I mean everyone except, of course, for the wealthy.

The wealthy tend to make more long-term decisions with their money. They spend less on the joys of today because they know they will benefit down the road. Wealthy people understand that the decisions they make today, negative or positive, will benefit them 5, 10, 15, and 20 years down the line. They have a vision for a better future and are willing to make sacrifices today to make that dream a reality.

The difference between the person I was during the 2008 market crash and who I am today is my ability to "see into" the future. Obviously not literally, but I'm willing to refrain from making unwise financial decisions in the present, all to gain as much as possible in the future. I do this by following the advice of the few who have achieved what I want to achieve, and avoiding the useless chatter of the majority. I'm willing to run opposite to my friends, family, and colleagues by understanding that no one can be wealthy in this world of gratification above all else.

KEY POINTS

- This is a world of short-term thinkers; stand apart from the crowd.
- Spend less on the joys of today, and focus on the joys that you can make possible for years in the future.
- Find mentors who think long-term, and learn how to "see into" the future like they do.

MONEY SMARTS

There Are People in This World Who Are Less Skilled Than You, Doing the Things That You Want to Do, Simply Because They Believe in Themselves.

They Also Take Action.

MONEY SMARTS

Building Wealth Isn't for Everyone.

Most of Your Family & Friends Will Never Understand What You're Trying to Achieve.

But Keep Going.

It's Worth It.

SECRET 4

Where Are You Headed? What is Your Destination?

"If you aim for nothing, you'll hit it every time."

— Unknown

Would you take a road trip without a destination in mind? If you did, would you ask other people to come along? Your passengers might have a few questions, like, *what direction are we headed in? How long will it take? What supplies do we need to pack on this journey? How much money should we bring?*

Taking a trip without being able to answer these questions would be silly. But this is how most people live their lives in terms of their finances. They have no roadmap or plan. They say they want to be wealthy, but never take the time to map out how to get there, or what wealth means to them. They somehow think that working extremely hard will result in massive wealth. That's the equivalent of driving really fast or for long hours, and expecting to reach a destination when you never selected one in the first place. Hustling your whole life for things that don't matter (traveling in the wrong direction) won't help you achieve wealth.

Sticking with the road trip analogy, let's say that "wealth" is the state of California, and is the destination of our road trip. You now have a few things to determine before planning your trip: *Where in the country are you currently? And what is the best route to get you to California?*

It's very difficult to map out directions to where you would like to go if you don't yet understand where you currently are. Your road trip to California would look a lot different if you left from Houston, Texas than if you departed from Boston. There are several planning tools you will want to have ready access to in order to establish your financial starting point. These include:

- Your personal (and/or spouse's) credit report
- Your personal or household monthly budget
- A list of all your assets and liabilities
- Your current net worth

Credit is everything on the journey toward building wealth. We will discuss how those with good credit build wealth much faster in Secret 9. I'll show you how having an 800-credit score is better than $500,000 cash.

If wealth is about maintaining a certain lifestyle regardless of the economic climate, then we first need to know what type of lifestyle you live or desire to live. That comes from creating and maintaining your family budget.

The easiest way to pull together a list of your assets and liabilities and determine your net worth is through personal financial software. I've been a big fan of Quicken for over fifteen years. Their intuitive software is easy to use and allows you to track these financial numbers efficiently, and more importantly, on a regular basis.

At the beginning of your road trip, you must have access to these financial maps. It would be a little premature in your trip-planning to make any final decisions without first understanding all of your possible starting points, routes, etc. We're going to revisit the roadmap a little later on, after we've discussed some basic wealth building strategies.

KEY POINTS

- Never hustle too hard without an idea of where you want to end up in the long run.
- If "wealth" is the state of California, from where in the world are you beginning your road trip? (Figure out where you stand before you make your itinerary). Never leave home without a map.
- Plot your course to wealth using the appropriate guiding tools: your credit score, your monthly household budget, a list of your current assets and liabilities, and your current net worth. Having these will help ensure that you have the right map for you.

SECRET 5

Income is NOT Wealth

"Buy land, they're not making it anymore."

—Mark Twain

What is wealth? In this book, I describe wealth as the ability to live one's lifestyle without interruption, regardless of the economic climate. Going further, wealth is being able to do what you want, regardless of the unemployment rate, the performance of the stock market, property values, or any other financial influence.

If you think about the above definition of wealth is shows how a person can have a very high income and still not be wealthy. It also shows how someone with a modest income can live a life of wealth. For example, if you live a lifestyle that is completely supported by $50,000 in annual income and you achieve that much or more from rental properties, you would be considered wealthy.

But if you live a lifestyle that requires $200,000 per year and have very little savings or passive income streams, you would not be considered wealthy. A high income can help you build wealth, but it is not wealth itself.

When thinking about wealth, take inventory of what you own. Do you work for others or for yourself? Is your income active or passive? How much of your time and energy goes into maintaining your lifestyle?

If the only thing you "own" is a job or a fixed amount of money, you will not be able to build real wealth.

As we continue, I'll show you how real estate can unlock not only a stream of passive income, but also an entirely new lifestyle if done right.

KEY POINTS

- If your income stream matches your desired lifestyle, you are wealthier than someone with more cash and a higher spending rate.
- A high income can help build wealth, but it is *not* wealth itself.
- You're wealthy when you can withstand changing financial tides e.g. stock market, property value, or unemployment rate swings without any negative impact on your lifestyle.

MONEY SMARTS

The Same Boiling Water That Softens a Potato Hardens an Egg.

It's About What You're Made Of. Not Your Circumstances.

MONEY SMARTS

Put Your Goals On Paper

80% Most People Don't Have Financial Goals.

13% Some People Have Goals in Their Heads.

2% Successful People Have Written Goals.

SECRET 6

Wealth Building is a Game. Do You Know Your Score?

"What you do today can improve all your tomorrows."

—Ralph Martson

I think the biggest mistake people make when trying to build wealth is not actively "keeping score". They say they want to be wealthy and make strategic moves, but how do they know where they are in the process? I look at wealth building like the game Monopoly. You're trying to collect paychecks and buy assets that provide you passive income, all while trying to stay out of jail. Real life isn't too much different.

So how do you keep score in real life? My favorite tool to organize my financial life is Quicken® software.

Quicken® is a money management tool you can use to track your financial well-being. I've been using this software for well over a decade and wouldn't be where I am today without it. It helps me track my income and expenses, and keeps it organized within personal, rental, and business categories.

The program then generates reports that indicate what areas of my finances are performing well and what ones need improvement. I can look at things on a monthly basis or year-to-year, easily trending how my income, net worth, and expenses have changed over time. This provides not just a snapshot but a full-scale portrait of my entire financial portfolio.

This touches on a common theme that you'll find throughout this book. Most people think that wealthy people somehow miraculously come into their good fortune, and then take certain measures afterwards to maintain their wealth, when it's actually a little more nuanced. Wealthy people take specific steps in order *to achieve their fortune AND to later build more wealth*.

Here's an example to help clarify my point. First, you should know that I love the game of basketball. When I was a freshman in high school, I wanted to play varsity basketball right out of the gate, but I didn't have a jump shot. In my mind, I was such a good player that I thought I should have immediately gotten the opportunity to play varsity and would work on my jump shot afterwards. Think about that. I was willing to put in the hard work to improve my jump shot, but only after I secured a spot on the varsity team. That was a silly way for a 15-year-old kid to think, and it of course turned out as you would imagine.

Yet, many of us as adults think or operate in a similar fashion. If I suggest that you subscribe to a money management program like Quicken®, you might immediately think, *"Right now, I have nothing to track. I'll get that after I have money."* Just like before, that's backwards thinking. If you don't track your progress, you won't know your score. If you don't know your score, how can you possibly foresee your next move?

A poor man thinks:

Once I get rich, I'll have good credit.

Once I have a lot of money, I'll start tracking it.

After I buy my first home, I'll cut out these bad spending habits.

A wealthy woman knows:

Good credit will lead to more income and opportunities.

The only way I'll become wealthy is knowing where my money is going, and that starts today.

If I stop these bad spending habits, I'll have enough for a down payment on my first home.

Treat your life like a company. Wealthy people know their numbers. What's your net worth (NW) today? If you don't know that number, you don't have a good handle on your finances. To keep things simple, you should think of your NW as your score in the wealth-building game.

High net worth won't directly lead to financial freedom, but it certainly helps. Your NW is equal to your total assets minus your total liabilities, so you should also know these two numbers.

Your net worth = [Total assets] – [Total liabilities]

Increasing your assets or reducing your liabilities increases your net worth. Conversely, increasing your liabilities or decreasing your assets diminishes your NW. If you're not familiar with that equation or those values, now would be a good time to please put this book down and spend a little time thinking about your numbers.

See the chart below for the average net worth of individuals by age bracket in America. You don't necessarily have to have the same goal, but for me, it's always been my goal to get into and stay in that top 1%.

Age of head of family	Median net worth	Average net worth
Less than 35	$13,900	$76,300
35-44	$91,300	$436,200
45-54	$168,600	$833,200
55-64	$212,500	$1,175,900
65-74	$266,400	$1,217,700
75+	$254,800	$977,600

Source: Nerdwallet.com 2020

Regardless of your goals, knowing your numbers is critical in the wealth building process. Remember, it's like playing a game of basketball; pay attention to the score to help you determine whether you should financially shoot, pass, or dribble out the clock.

Here's how you find your net worth: use financial software like Quicken® to track all of your assets, meaning everything that you own like properties, stocks, bonds, etc. You should also track all of your liabilities, AKA everything that you owe someone else. The software will compute your net worth number. This is your "wealth building score".

Use any financial planning software that you'd like - other great tools include Microsoft Money® or Mint® - just as long as you're tracking your finances to create a clear picture of your current portfolio.

KEY POINTS

- Treat your life like a company - know your net worth.
- Find a financial tracking tool like Quicken® to determine your NW or financial score.
- Don't make plans for after you're wealthy, make plans to *become* wealthy.

Section 2

Set Yourself Up For Success

SECRET 7

Money Today is Worth Less Than Yesterday

"Inflation today is the crabgrass in your savings."

—Robert Orben

Micro- and macroeconomics were 2 of my favorite college courses. It was eye-opening for me to see how money flows into the economy and how smart investors make decisions based on certain economic indicators.

Most people understand inflation at its most basic form, but don't truly understand how it affects our lives at a higher level. Each of us as consumers has an individual "basket of goods" quota. It includes the items that we buy or consume on a regular basis, such as food, clothing, transportation, and even entertainment.

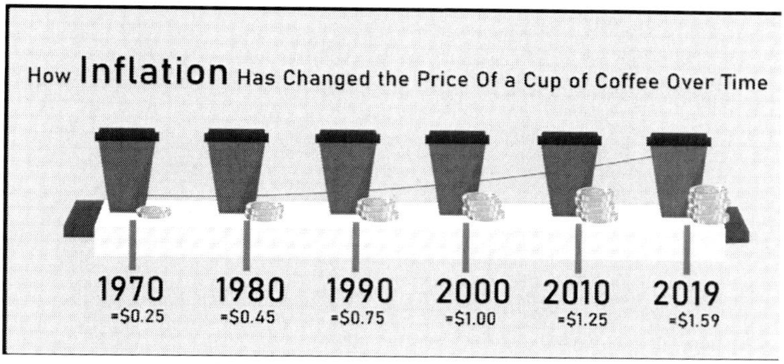

As the above graphic suggests, the prices of these and all other goods steadily increase year after year, which is known as *inflation*. Inflation eats away at the purchasing power of a dollar. That hard-earned $100 of yours essentially buys fewer goods today than it could five years ago, and furthermore will buy even less five years from now.

Going further, let's suppose that the inflation rate (the amount that your basket of goods increases in price) is 2% per year. If you put $100 into the piggy bank on your nightstand and leave it there for one year, that same $100 becomes worthless, in a sense. While the monetary value is still the same, the price of your basket of goods has gone up to $102. Your $100 in savings has lost purchasing power. So, what do you do with that money instead of putting it in your piggy bank?

Most people would then think the obvious solution would be to put the money into a bank savings account. There are many flaws with that strategy, but the simple answer is no. You'd be lucky to keep pace with the rate of inflation. I'm not sure if it's intentionally set up this way, but in my experience, banks do not provide savings interest rates that meet or exceed the inflation rate. Thus, your money would essentially sit in a savings account instead of your piggy bank, and still not allow you to purchase your "basket of goods". Just keeping pace with inflation rate is a shortsighted goal anyhow.

Your true goal should be to make money with your money. This means investing it with a return that exceeds the inflation rate. If you put that same $100 into an investment that returns you 6% for the year, now you have a true net gain of 4%: 6% return on investment against a -2% inflation rate. Your money would be making more money with minimal effort on your part, and that is the true goal of every wealthy person.

By now you may have realized that your salary is also combating inflation. Without a cost of living increase from your job, your salary would buy fewer goods than it could the year before. I hear many people say, "I just can't seem to get ahead," and this internal feeling may come from their consistent loss in purchasing power. A $75,000 salary with a 2% raise every year means you're making more money, but if inflation is also at 2%, you have not increased your purchasing power, and you haven't gotten ahead. Most people will never get ahead by simply working a job. This is why the wealthy put so much time into finding great investments, to maintain or increase their purchasing power. The wealthy want their money working hard for them, and so should you.

KEY POINTS

- Understand the relationship between your purchasing power and yearly inflation.
- Don't depend solely on savings to beat inflation; find smart investment opportunities.
- Make your money work hard for you, so you don't have to.

MONEY SMARTS

People Don't Like Starting Something New Because to the Outside World They Appear to Be Starting From the Bottom.

The Opinions of Others Are Holding You Back.

MONEY SMARTS

Most People Don't Want to Risk 2-5 Years of Their Life Learning to Invest in Real Estate Because it's Too Risky.

They Would Rather Spend 40-50 Years Working for a Company That Will Lay Them Off as Soon as the Economy Cools Down.

And That's Safe?

SECRET 8

You Can't Save Your Way to a Healthy Retirement: Investing is a MUST

"How many millionaires do you know who have become wealthy by investing in savings accounts? I rest my case."

–Robert G. Allen

I have 2 major problems with the way most Americans plan for their lives in retirement, but before we tackle these issues, let's discuss a few important figures that will help to illustrate my points.

In 2019, the average American's salary was just under $50,000 annually.[1] Let's use this as a benchmark for our conversation. Let's also assume that $1,000,000 is your retirement savings goal and

---

[1] Source: U.S. Bureau of Labor Statistics Latest Numbers – BLS.gov

your plan is to call it quits professionally at the age of 65. This is a lofty goal considering that the average 60-year-old has roughly $200,000 in retirement savings, but let's keep that $1 million figure in mind for now.

If you're the average American, you likely save 10% of your income (or $5000 per year) and achieve a consistent return on investment of 6.5% in your 401k. At this rate, it would take roughly 40 years to save up $1 million.

You might say, "*But wait, I'll receive several raises over that 40-year period and my salary wouldn't stay at $50,000.*"

Okay, let's imagine you have an incredible job where your employer gives raises that exceed the rate of inflation, and you somehow shave five years off this timeline. It would still take you at least 35 years to get to your big goal of $1,000,000.

With that in mind, let's consider some scenarios in which this typical retirement planning approach would leave you short-changed.

Scenario 1:

You've been working for 35 years and your retirement account has just hit the $1,000,000 mark. Congrats! You're finally ready to retire when *BOOM*—the stock market crashes.

In 2020 (and earlier in 2007), I personally saw some retirement accounts slashed by 40% or more. What happens if in the year you decide to retire, or a couple years after you retire, you take a 40% hit to your savings? That $1,000,000 you thought you had safely stashed away is now just $600,000. You'd likely be unsure of the economic climate and what to do. In 2007, many older Americans were forced to return to the workforce or significantly changed their lifestyles to meet their new realities.

Scenario 2:

Let's look at the same scenario with a twist. Imagine that everything proceeds as you planned with regard to your retirement, but right before the stock market crashes, you liquidate your $1,000,000 and put all your funds into a safe money market account. *Whew. That was close!* You're no longer achieving a 6.5% return on your money, but your cash is at least safe.

Now let's say the money market mirrors the inflation rate and your million-dollar savings continues to have the equivalent purchasing power into your retirement years. If you continue to live a $50,000 lifestyle, you essentially have 20 years before you run out of retirement savings. Let's put this into perspective: you started saving for retirement at age 30, and 35 years later, you have 1 million bucks. You're 65 years old and would now like to retire. But if you live past age 85, you won't have any money left.

Sadly, this will be the reality for the majority of us. My great grandmother lived until she was 103 years old, and that was back in the 80s. Modern medicine is helping us to live even longer, and if you only have enough savings for 20 years, then you are setting yourself up to likely burden someone else in the future.

Here is the push-back I typically receive when I discuss these figures with others:

"I'll just start saving earlier and work until I'm 75".

My response would be, okay, but the numbers still don't play out very well. I would argue that you would now be giving up 40-50 of your best years working instead of enjoying life.

"I'll just spend less money in my retirement years than I did in my working years to make my money last longer."

If you think that's realistic, let me ask you this: Right now, do you spend more money during the week or on the weekends? I would argue that the weekends consume more of your money, as you have more leisure time on your hands.

So, once you retire, wouldn't every day be a weekend? How could you possibly plan to spend less? Do you think you could spend 30-40 years living like a miser to save up $1 million, only to continue living that way in your retirement? That does not sound like a great life.

I'm not suggesting that you shouldn't contribute to your job's 401k savings plan. The opposite is actually true; I think you should contribute, and to the max, especially if your employer has a match program. You should contribute enough to get the full benefit.

I also think that you should start saving as early as possible, as the compounding effects of savings (especially pre-tax) is a wonderful thing.

What I do NOT recommend is that you rely solely on this savings account as your only retirement vehicle. It is foolish to believe that your 401k fund will allow you to live a comfortable retirement. I would also encourage you to invest outside of your 401k in more tangible assets that you can control.

Your retirement goal should be to create multiple streams of passive income. I'm a huge fan of cash-flowing real estate as an investment vehicle because it helps address the issues mentioned above. Real estate can continue to pay you month after month throughout your retirement so that you won't have to worry about catastrophic market changes or outliving your savings.

Though the value of your real estate may drop during a recession, the income stream from rental units will typically stay unchanged or may even increase during a bad economy.

Before we move on, I have a challenge for you. Find 5 people in retirement that are living the lifestyle you want to live when you retire. Ask them what they did to achieve this awesome feat and see how you can emulate it. Always keep your definition of wealth in mind as you plan for your future.

KEY POINTS

- Just relying on your savings alone is not enough to secure your retirement.
- Contribute to your 401k, but don't depend on it. Find other tangible assets in which to invest.
- Set up multiple passive income streams, such as collecting rent, to keep you afloat in retirement.

SECRET 9

Credit is King

"Successful people do what unsuccessful people are not willing to do. Don't wish it were easier; wish you were better."

— Jim Rohn

Would you rather have an 800 FICO score or $1 million in your hands right now? What if you take the $1 million and your FICO score permanently dropped below 600?

If you chose the 800-credit score, it's most likely because you understand the power of leverage. In Secret 21, we will talk a little bit further about monetary leverage, but for right now, let's focus on the concept of credit itself.

Your FICO score is an indicator of how much risk is associated with lending you credit, and is based on a few factors like timeliness of debt repayment, the number of lines of credit you have open, etc. For now, it should suffice for you to know that a higher credit score implies that there would be less risk for a lender to give you credit, and vice versa.

Most people assume that wealthy people have good credit because they have money to pay their bills. This is true, but the relationship between wealth and credit is more interrelated. Good credit helps you become wealthy by providing you access to money, which in turn allows you to buy assets. It is key to understand that you don't actually have to have the cash in hand in order to buy these assets, but can do so on the basis of a strong credit score. Buying assets that are profitable then allows the wealthy to pay their debts on time, which further strengthens their credit. Wealthy people protect their personal credit scores because they know the difference between scores of 650 and 750 represents hundreds of thousands of possible spending dollars or more during their lifetime.

$20,000 Car Loan Paid Over 5 Years

Credit Score	Interest Rate	Monthly Paymen	Additional Cost of Bad Credit (5 Years)
720 Or Above	4.9%	$ 367.51	$ -
680-719 Score	7.0%	$ 396.02	$ 1,170.49
620- 679 Score	9.0%	$ 415.17	$ 2,319.46
580-619	19.0%	$ 518.81	$ 8,538.20
579 - Below	29.0%	$ 634.84	$ 15,499.43

Multiply the cost x 10 vehicles that the average person will own during their lifetime.

200,000 Mortgage Loan Paid Over 30 Years

Credit Score	Interest Rate	Monthly Paymen	Additional Cost of Bad Credit (30 Years)
720 Or Above	5.90%	$ 1,073.64	$ -
680-719 Score	7.50%	$ 1,398.43	$ 116,924.40
620- 679 Score	8.50%	$ 1,537.83	$ 167,108.40
580-619	9.90%	$ 1,740.38	$ 240,026.40
579 - Below	12.00%	$ 2,057.23	$ 354,092.40

Check out the numbers below. It shows lifetime savings for home and auto purchases over the lifespans of two separate individuals: one with a good credit score and one with a bad credit score. It is important to note that these metrics don't include the difference in savings on multiple credit cards, personal loans, or other forms of financing.

An individual a life of bad credit (579 or below) can pay close to 1/2 million dollars in additional interest cost over somone with a 720 score.

10 Vehicle Purchases = $150,499.00 in additional interest charges
1 Home Purchases = 354,092.00
Total Cost of Financing a life with bad credit = $504,591

When you take care of your credit, the cost of money is significantly decreased. If you take the savings and also reinvest at a rate of 5% per year, that number grows even more. I currently spend $45 a month to have access to all three of my scores and credit reports. I receive email alerts for every inquiry and new account that hits my report. With bad credit, you may be able to become temporarily rich, but you'll never become wealthy.

When I speak about credit at seminars, I often tell people that I've never been to North Dakota. I don't have any contacts or family members in that area either. However, if you took all of my financial resources away and put me in the middle of North Dakota with nothing but my credit score, I would be back "on top" in no time.

In Secret 42, we will talk about business credit. We'll explore how you can multiply your wealth using not only your personal credit but the credit profile of one or multiple businesses as well. That's where your wealth can grow exponentially.

How to Quickly Improve Your Credit Score:

- Pay down your credit cards and keep below 40% of your credit limit
- Avoid applying for new accounts too frequently
- Add someone else's credit history to your profile

- Find a co-signer for your loan
- Diversify your credit profile
- Get a secured line of credit
- Get your credit limit increased with current lenders
- Get creditors to update positive info after you pay
- Get a free credit report at AnnualCreditReport.com

Achieving a (near) perfect credit score doesn't happen overnight, but taking any of the actions listed above can make drastic differences in your ability to leverage additional resources to help build your wealth. It has long been said that cash is king, but in my opinion if you want to realistically secure your financial future, striving for good credit is far more worthwhile.

KEY POINTS

- In the long run, credit is more valuable than cash.
- Good credit provides access to cheaper financing, which in turn provides access to cheaper assets.
- Keep regular track of your credit and you will save tons of cash over your lifetime

MONEY SMARTS

How is My Credit Score Determined?

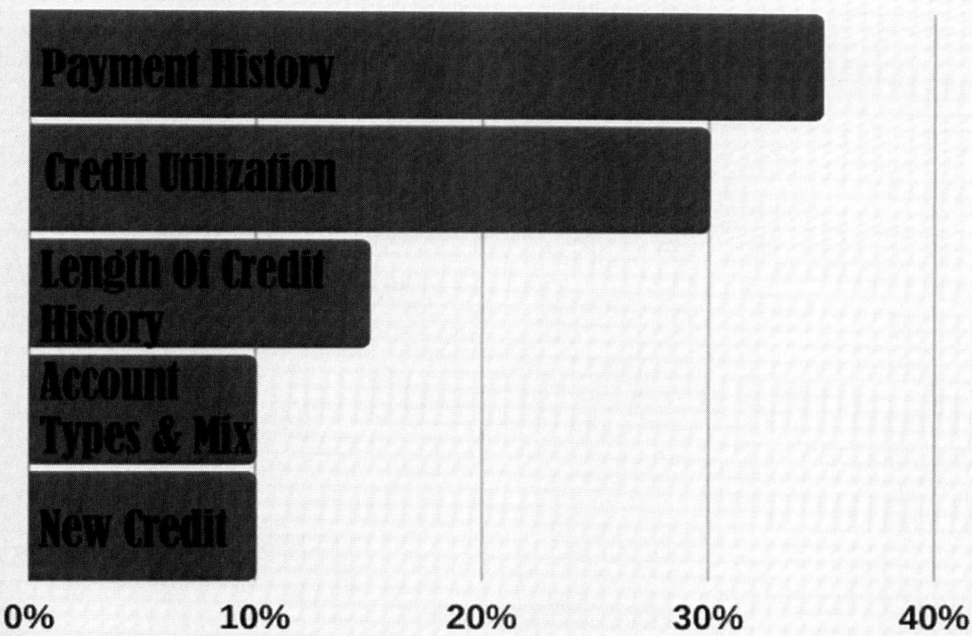

MONEY SMARTS

If Something Costs $100 & You Buy It On Sale For 25% Off, You Didn't Save $25.

You Simply Spent $75.

SECRET 10

Homeownership is Still a Smart Move

"I will forever believe that buying a home is a great investment. Why? Because you can't live in a stock certificate. You can't live in a mutual fund."

— Oprah Winfrey

I bought my first home at age 23 and it was probably one of the smartest things I've ever done. I don't look at my personal residence as an investment, but I do look at it as a valuable asset. Here's how homeownership could help you secure your financial future.

First, you can control your cost. A nice 30-year fixed-rate mortgage allows you to expect similar living costs year after year. Your taxes and insurance may go up as the value of the property goes up, but the principal and interest, or the larger part of your mortgage, stay where they are for the life of the loan. You also won't have to worry about yearly rent hikes by any landlords.

Homeownership also offers flexibility in your payment schedule. If you choose to, you can accelerate the payments and pay off your mortgage sooner. This would leave just taxes and insurance to pay, and ultimately reduce your overall monthly living expenses. You could also do this several years down the line with a simple refinance of the mortgage.

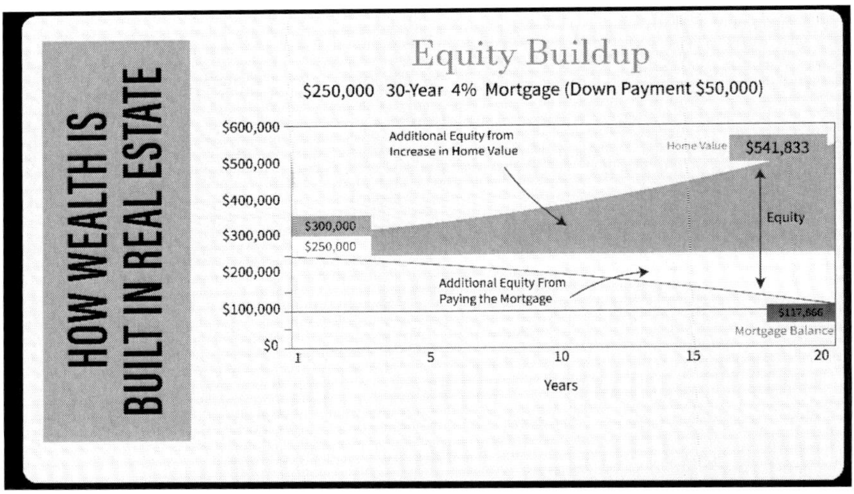

For instance, if you own your home for 7 years and run into financial trouble, you may want to reduce your monthly expenses. You could refinance your mortgage, spreading the principal balance once again over 30 years, thus decreasing your monthly principal and interest payment. Of course, this would increase the time over which you pay off the loan and increase your interest expense, but you would still have the option of making additional payments once your financial situation has stabilized. The beauty of ownership is the range of options it allows you to utilize based on your circumstances.

Ownership also offers many tax benefits not necessarily given to tenants. The address on my mortgage is currently tax-deductible, as are the property taxes that I pay. Additionally, I can run my business from a home office. This allows me to write off a portion of my insurance, utilities, Internet, etc. that is associated with running that business, and is proportional to the amount of space that the business occupies in my home.

Don't have a home business? Well, you should. We'll talk about that in a bit.

Your home can also make you money. Do you have an extra bedroom or the ability to furnish the basement? This extra space could represent a great source of passive rental income. I have clients who rent out several bedrooms in their homes, and have their entire mortgages paid by these tenants. Others rent spare bedrooms to international students seeking safe, affordable housing for the duration of their programs of study.

Maybe you'd rather not have roommates or boarders? Instead, you could list your entire house on Airbnb when you're out of town, and have a segment of your monthly expenses paid by these travelers.

While I wouldn't consider buying a condo or single-family home to be an investment, buying a multi-unit home or multi-family home is a different story. This can be a great investment for a first-time home buyer. Specifically, you could use a government-sponsored loan with very little cash out of pocket, and the return on your investment even within a few years would be incredible. I will address multi-family homes and the basics of real estate investing in the next section.

KEY POINTS

- A fixed rate mortgage beats monthly rent in the long run.
- Ownership gives you options to either pay off your mortgage early or refinance the mortgage to help distribute the costs in ways that work for you.
- A multi-family home can be bought with very little cash out of pocket, and leasing out extra rooms can help pay for it.

SECRET 11

Your Time, Money, & Resources are Limited – Choose Wisely

"A pessimist sees the difficulty in every opportunity; an optimist sees the opportunity in every difficulty."

— Winston Churchill

Are you the type of person to seize what's in front of you, or wait for something better? Is the potential of a bigger reward tomorrow worth passing up a smaller one today? Regardless, these situations represent another important wealth-building concept: *opportunity cost.* Simply put, opportunity cost is what you "give up" in pursuit of something else. It is best explained by the following 2 examples:

Imagine you could invest $1000 today and earn 50% on your money. This in turn would yield $1500 in one year. Alternatively, you have the opportunity to take the $1000 and buy a 4K flat-screen TV. You can't do both because your funds are limited, but you want to do something. Either way, the opportunity cost would be the missed potential of not choosing the other course i.e. not having an extra $500 in one year vs. not being able to enjoy high-definition in-home entertainment.

Here's what you should realize though. If you bought the TV, it didn't cost you $1000. It really cost you $1500, or your original amount of cash plus the $500 in interest that you missed out on by foregoing the investment opportunity.

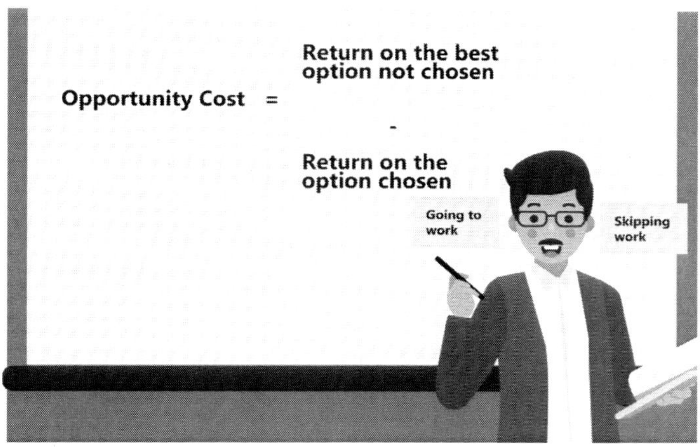

Opportunity cost also applies to your time. We're all given the same 24 hours in a day and our respective successes or failures depend on what we do with that time. If you spend one hour reading this book, you may have given up one hour of watching TV or exercising, but hopefully you have found as much utility in learning about wealth-building as you would relaxing vs. staying fit.

Almost everything we do and purchase has an opportunity cost, something that should be considered when you decide to spend money or invest. Even when you commit to investing your time and money, funds will be limited. Long-term, as your real estate portfolio grows, remember to only dedicate time and money on the wisest and most profitable investments.

KEY POINTS

- Opportunity cost is what you give up in pursuit of something else.
- When purchasing something now instead of investing for later, the opportunity cost is the interest growth that you sacrificed for short term gain.
- Opportunity cost also applies to time, so spend your time as wisely as you would your money.

MONEY SMARTS

Saving Vs Investing

& The Power Of Compound Interest

Saving 20$ Per Day For The Next 35 Years Yields

$264,000.00

Investing $20 Per Day (@ A Rate Of 7%) For The Next 35 Years Yields

$1,028,695.91

MONEY SMARTS

The Truth is This... Rich People Stay Rich by Living Like They're Broke. Broke People Stay Broke by Living Like They're Rich.

SECRET 12

What's Done is Done

"Perhaps the secret to making a billion dollars in real estate is that there is no secret."

— David Lichtenstein

I was recently introduced to a new accountant by a mutual acquaintance. Based on everything that I had heard from my colleague, this accountant appeared to be a big shot in the field. My hope was that he would save me thousands of dollars in my business and taxes, and so I gave him a $1500 retainer, as he requested, to begin our work relationship.

Unfortunately, from our very first interaction, he rubbed me the wrong way. I didn't feel like he was someone who I could trust with my money. He requested an additional $300 not long after he started working for me, and his prices had increased from his initial quote.

In this situation, the money that I had paid to this accountant was a *sunk cost*. Sunk cost is money you've spent that can't be recovered. I believe that humans are emotional beings at core. Even when we're trying to be logical, we still interject some emotion into our decisions. This emotion can lead us to justify our current spending based on our past actions or sentiments.

So in regards to the accountant, the retainer money was gone and I wasn't able to recover it. But I didn't let my emotions overrule and cause me to give him more money to justify what I'd already spent and continue to wait for the outstanding work I'd heard about. Instead, I decided to cut ties and find a new accountant. I also paid the second $300 invoice to keep my professional name pristine and to not burn any bridges.

Emotionally, it was difficult to get over, but I know that that spent money really shouldn't have been a factor when deciding what was my next best financial move. At the end of the day, sunk cost money will never return, and you shouldn't justify future spending on the basis of potential improvement in the situation.

Sunk Cost Fallacy

Sunk cost fallacy makes us continue a venture or behavior & pursue an inferior alternative simply becuase we have invested resources previously.

KEY POINTS

- Sunk cost money is money spent that cannot be recovered.
- Do not justify future costs based on sunk costs.
- If you spend money on a bad deal, swallow the sunk costs. Don't pay further into the situation for the sake of ego or emotions.

Section 3

Create Your Game Winning Strategy

SECRET 13

Understand What You Can For Yourself

"Buy when everyone else is selling and hold until everyone else is buying. That's not just a catchy slogan. It's the very essence of successful investing."

— J. Paul Getty

By now, you hopefully understand that inflation is eating away at your purchasing power and that you need to be investing in assets that perform at or above the rate of inflation.

What are the factors that you need to consider when choosing an investment? How much money should you invest? What's a good return on your investment?

Here are a few pieces of advice and a quick crash course on financial advising. First, I think everyone should be their own financial advisor. Ultimately, you shouldn't be putting your money in someone else's hands and relying on them to secure your financial future. You don't have to become a professional stock trader, but you should understand the basics and know what questions to ask about any investment.

Get familiar with the idea of *liquidity*. It sounds like a term from science class, but actually refers to how quickly you can turn an investment back into cash. Stocks are a great example of liquidity because you can usually get rid of your shares within any given trading day. Real estate is an *illiquid* (not very liquid) investment, as it would take more time (typically between 30 to 90 days) to return your property to cash.

Then there are *holding periods*. Anytime you're interested in a new investment, you should think about your holding period or how long you plan to keep that particular investment. This concept features heavily in your personal *investment timeline.*

For example, suppose you're 25-years-old and investing into a retirement account. Your investment timeline is roughly 40 years, assuming that your goal retirement age is 65. With a 40-year timeline, you might be less concerned about the ebb and flow of the market. You would likely consider investments that are long-term plays. This doesn't necessarily mean that your holding period would span the entire 40 years, but it does mean you could be less concerned with the short-term performance.

Lastly, avoid *speculation*. Allow me to tell a brief story to better illustrate this concept.

I'll never forget the day when a young woman came into my real estate office hoping to invest in a condo in a pretty pricey neighborhood. At the time, she mentioned that she planned to move from Boston to California in a couple of years. My agent asked her why she wanted to buy a home when she wasn't going to stick around in it for very long. Her answer blew me away. She explained that the price of condos in that neighborhood had been climbing in value by 10% per year for the past few years. She intended to use the majority of her liquid cash to buy the condo, hold it for 2 years, and earn an additional $50,000 when she eventually sold it and moved to California.

I hope you see the flaw in her plan. But if you can't, let me clarify: this is **not** investing. This is pure speculation, meaning that she assumed that the real estate market would continue to appreciate like it had over the previous 2 years. However, there's no guarantee that the real estate market would continue to uptrend during her 2-year holding period; there's also no assurance that prices wouldn't fall. And so, her rationale (and her investment) becomes more tenuous.

This would've been a great home for her if she had planned to stay long-term, but a silly investment decision. When you invest in real estate, invest for cash flow, **not** for possible appreciation. Keep in mind that appreciation will likely occur, but it's simply the icing and not the entire cake.

KEY POINTS

- Understand whether your investments are liquid or illiquid.
- Always know your holding period, or how long you plan to retain a particular investment.
- Don't speculate! Buy real estate for cash flow, not market appreciation; appreciation is the icing on the cake.

SECRET 14

You Can't Control the Markets

"The individual investor should act consistently as an investor and not as a speculator."

— Benjamin Graham

My goal for you is to gain a better understanding of wealth-building through real estate, but before we start talking about real estate investments, I think it would be worthwhile to discuss more traditional avenues of generating passive income. The average person is more likely to be familiar with investments in stocks and bonds as opposed to real estate, and possibly the risks and benefits of each.

Above all, when you invest in a stock, a bond, or a mutual fund, understand that someone else controls how well each one does. Before I advise you on how to play this to your advantage though, let's review the basics.

Buying Stock in a Company

There are multiple ways to put your money in the market, the simplest of which is a *stock purchase*. Stocks are securities that represent some degree of ownership in a company. If you purchase the stock of a specific company, like McDonald's, you essentially hold a small stake in the company in exchange for the capital that you paid for the stock.

Sometimes, a company will decide to combine stocks. They can merge multiple stocks, 10 for example, into a single share: this would increase the amount per share by a factor of 10, and all those investors who had fewer than this amount would lose their stakes in the company. This is 1 way in which stock purchases are controlled by the company and not you the investor.

Buying Bonds

An alternative to a stock purchase would be to purchase a bond. Bonds are similar to loans, but with some key features. With a bond, you loan your money to the government or a municipality (city) in the present, and in exchange, they'll repay your loan at some point in the future. The fine details regarding when they will repay you the loaned funds - *the bond principal* - and how much interest they'll pay – *the coupon* - are set by the government or city.

Purchasing into Mutual Funds

Another investment vehicle related to stock purchases are mutual funds. You can think of a mutual fund as a team effort for the purchase of stocks or bonds. Basically, your money is pooled with money from other investors into a fund, which then invests in certain securities according to a stated investment strategy. The fund is overseen by a *fund manager* who reports to a board of directors. Therefore, when you invest in a mutual fund, the fund manager is controlling the outcome.

At the end of the day, the best way to make money from the stock market is to participate in it in different ways and to always make sure to diversify your investments.

When it comes to participation, you're probably already doing it: most employers will invest part of your paycheck into a 401k, or if you work in a non-profit or for a government employer, they'll invest in a 403b.

Beyond what your employer invests, though, it's wise to have your own private account on a brokerage site like Fidelity. This gives you leeway to pick out companies that you've researched and believe in. Once you've acquired a certain amount of money and liquidity, you can hire a stock broker, who will do a lot of the heavy lifting for you. This once again takes your finances out of your control, so always practice caution.

As I mentioned earlier, don't skew too heavily in one industry and make sure to diversify. For instance, if you were to only invest entirely in airlines like JetBlue, your whole portfolio would've crashed during the COVID-19 pandemic. If you had invested in the Minnesota Mining & Manufacturing Corporation, also known as 3M, though, you would've made quite a bit of money. If you had invested in both, you would've probably stayed relatively stable. In this case, stability is preferable, because you don't know if one day 3M will end up crashing and JetBlue will end up booming.

When things are out of your control, it's best to have other income sources to help offset the risk.

KEY POINTS

- Real estate investment is a lesser known option for wealth building compared to more traditional avenues like purchasing stocks, bonds, or mutual funds.
- Spread your investments out among stocks, bonds, and mutual funds; don't invest in just one industry.
- Diversify your portfolio to minimize risk.

MONEY SMARTS

Is Real Estate Right for Me?

During the Last Two Hundred Years, About 90 Percent of The World's Millionaires Have Created Their Wealth by Investing in Real Estate.

MONEY SMARTS

How Much Money Am I Wasting Making My Landlord Rich?

Rent	Year 1	Year 5	Year 10	Year 15
$700	$8400	$42k	$84k	$126k
$1000	$12k	$60k	$120k	$180k
$1500	$18k	$90k	$180k	$270k
$2000	$24k	$120k	$240	$360k

SECRET 15

More is Sometimes More: Make Smarter Investments with Multi-Family Properties

"Ninety percent of all millionaires become so through owning real estate."

—Andrew Carnegie

From my early experiences at the car dealership and later through my college coursework, I came to understand economics and realized that I needed to keep growing my income and net worth despite inflation. If my income wasn't growing at least as quickly as the rate of inflation, then my money was losing its purchasing power. I also learned that money sitting idly in a savings account was worth less every day. Overall, the faster my money could move and make money for me, the faster I would get to financial freedom. This is a true secret of the wealthy, and so they are always looking for ways to invest their money.

Recall that net worth is equal to your assets minus your liabilities, and that growing your net worth requires you to increase your assets and/or reduce your liabilities. This is why I love real estate investing so much. When I buy a house and place it for rent each month, my tenants pay me money, which I in turn use to pay my mortgage. With each mortgage payment the principal balance is reduced my a small amount, which reduces my liability amount and increases my net worth. I've become wealthier with each passing month simply from debt reduction paid by someone else.

Simple economics tells us that real estate prices will likely increase as time goes on. It goes back to supply and demand. There is a limited supply of land and thus space upon which to build real estate, yet our population continues to grow. Like with any commodity, a dwindling supply combined with increasing demand tends to drive prices upward. There will certainly be minor economic dips, and parts of the country where population growth won't be as robust, but on the whole, prices for land will trend upward over the long haul.

Appreciation is the term used to describe the increase in real estate prices. This works in your favor when you own property. Going back to our net worth equation, as your property appreciates, your assets increase, therefore growing your net worth. As you can see from the chart below, you can use appreciation and passive debt payment simultaneously to your advantage and make you wealthy.

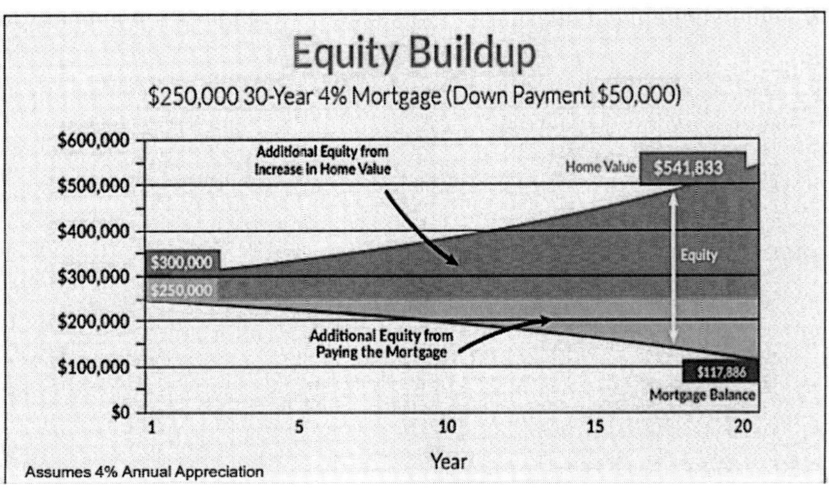

One of the greatest benefits of real estate investment is the ability to take control of an asset with a large amount of leverage. With residential real estate, you can take control of a $100,000 investment with just $3500 out of your pocket. This might sound unbelievable, but it is possible through a Federal Housing Administration (FHA) loan, which allows you to contribute as low as a 3.5% down payment at the time of purchase.

Let's take a step back and think about what an amazing opportunity this could be: you basically reap the benefits of controlling a piece of property, but have not yet paid for that asset entirely. This is leverage at its best. At the higher end, you may need to put down between $20,000 to $25,000 to gain control of a $100,000 asset. This still outweighs any other investment, including stocks. Comparatively, you would have to put down at least $50,000 to control $100,000 in stocks as stocks require a 50% margin (down payment) to purchase in a best-case scenario.

Going further, buying a multi-family home increases your investment performance in many cases. This is where I encourage all of my first-time investor clients to start if they don't already own a home. The ability to use government-backed loans to buy up to 4 units is a powerful tool. This is how my wife and I got started. To be clear, my wife is not in the real estate game and has a fulfilling career in healthcare. Before we married and moved in together, she acted on my advice, and bought a 3-family home with a small down payment; I did the same. We lived separately, and our respective tenants paid the majority of our bills. After the wedding, we decided to buy the single-family home that we really wanted all along. We were able to buy this property with a 5% down payment out of our pockets. This is an owner-occupied residential mortgage. Altogether, we now own our primary residence and 6 additional rental units that we keep as investment properties. The best part is that all of these were purchased with very little money that she and I actively worked for.

So, I would argue that to maximize your use of an occupied lending, consider buying a multi-family home first. If we had bought our single-family first and later attempted to invest in 3-family homes, then the lenders would've asked us for 20 to 25% down at purchase. But because we prioritized buying the multi-families as owner-occupied properties, we took advantage of relatively low-down payment government-backed loans. If you're interested in a similar opportunity, I would recommend that you talk to your local mortgage broker for the most current information regarding your options.

\Whatever type of home you choose to buy as an investment property though, be sure that you have carefully weighed the *cash flow* potential. Cash flow is the difference between your property's monthly income(s) and its monthly expenses. The income would be the total amount of payment in rent that you receive from the property. Your expenses would be the total cost of that property and anything spent to maintain it i.e. the mortgage payment, taxes, insurance, water, sewage, property management if you choose, and maintenance. Think of it as anything you would need to ensure a safe, clean environment for your tenant(s). If done properly, your investment property could net you a considerable amount of money each month without you even breaking a sweat. Remember that your real estate investment is only as valuable as its cash flow potential.

KEY POINTS

- Real estate is an asset that can yield great leverage for investors in exchange for very little out-of-pocket costs.
- As your properties appreciate in value, your net worth likewise increases. Similarly, owning a rental property can help reduce your liabilities and thus grow your net worth.
- Purchasing a multi-family home as a rental property before buying a single-family home allows you to take advantage of government-backed loans.

MONEY SMARTS

If You Want To Become a Member of The

1%

You Must Be Willing to Do What The Other 99% Are Not.

SECRET 16

Your Money Should Always be Working Hard For You

"You don't have to be too bright to get into real estate."

— David Lichtenstein

When it comes to refinancing, home-equity loans, and lines of credit, I find that there are really no hard and fast rules. Deciding when to utilize these options comes down to your strategy, where you are in the market cycle, and the best move to get you to your goals. The important thing is that you know these tools are available to you and how to use them. Just like a chef won't need a whisk for every meal that he makes, he still knows that that tool is available given the right occasion.

Let's say you have a rental property that's worth $400,000, and your current mortgage balance, what you owe, is $200,000. Assuming there are no other loans on the property, you have $200,000 in equity and you're at roughly a 50% loan-to-value ratio. This means you owe 50% of what the home is worth.

We'll continue to use this particular property in our discussion below to demonstrate how to tap into that $200,000 of equity. Let's also assume that your mortgage payment (principal, interest, taxes, insurance) is $2000 per month, other expenses are $500 per month, and your interest rate is 6%. Last, let's assume that you're collecting $4000 monthly in rental income, resulting in a net cash flow of about $1500. This is where your specific goals and strategy will come into play. Again, not every tool is useful in every situation, but one or more of the following options may be useful to you in the future.

Straight Refinance

Refinancing is simply getting a new loan to pay off the old loan. You may refinance with the same bank or a new lender altogether. For example, if market interest rates have dropped to 4%, it may be a good time for you to refinance your existing loan. Given the 6% rate from above, the new 4% interest rate would drastically reduce your monthly mortgage payments.

Another method of refinancing is to renegotiate the time over which the loan is paid. Stretching out the loan over 30 years would obviously decrease your monthly payments, but extends your debt timeframe. So why would you do this? Why wouldn't you just pay off the loan as quickly as possible? This goes back to your personal finance strategy and goals. If you want to increase your cash flow today, then this may work for you. As your monthly mortgage payments shrink, and assuming other factors stay the same, then your cash flow number grows. Put another way, if refinancing the loan decreased your monthly payment by $400, you will now see a reciprocal boost in your cash flow.

Cash-Out Refinance

In this situation, let's start with the same circumstances as in the example above, but now we want to take money out of the property for some other use. Most bank lenders on an investment property will allow up to a 75% loan-to-value ratio. This typically means that you can borrow up to 75% of what the property is worth.

From above, our rental property is worth $400,000, so we should be able to borrow up to $300,000 on this property ($400,000× 0.75). This means we should be able to tap into $100,000 in cash with a cash-out refinance. If we took out $100,000 and increased our new loan to $300,000, our mortgage payments would increase but would still be well covered by our rental income. Our cash flow number will decrease because of the additional debt, however we now have $100,000 in hand to do with whatever we choose.

If you chose to reinvest this money, you could use this as a down payment on an identical investment property. You've now increased your cash flow, have two mortgages that you're simultaneously paying down with rental income, and own $800,000 in properties that are hopefully appreciating in value.

Home-Equity Loan vs Home-Equity Line of Credit

Let's consider another scenario using the same figures. Your home is still worth $400,000, but let's say that in this particular market, interest rates have increased to 8%. If your home loan balance of $200,000 is financed at 6%, it likely would not be a good idea to refinance the entire loan at a higher interest rate.

Now imagine that you were looking to tap into your equity for some purpose. It would thus make more sense to do a home-equity loan as opposed to a second mortgage. You would keep your first mortgage of $200,000 in place. Your interest rate would stay at 6%, and your payments would remain the same. If you took out an additional mortgage on the property for $100,000, it would be at the new market rate of 8%. Overall, having two mortgages with different interest rates would be less expensive than having the entire $300,000 loan at 8%.

With a home-equity loan, the bank will give you $100,000 in one lump sum. You start making principal and interest payments on the entire amount immediately.

A home-equity line of credit (HELOC) is similar to a home equity loan, and is generally a second position mortgage. In most cases, you keep your first mortgage in place and take out a second mortgage to tap into the equity within the home. Unlike with a home equity loan, the equity from a HELOC is disbursed like a credit card. Instead of the bank giving you a lump sum check of $100,000 at the closing, they would give you a checkbook with access to that amount of money as you need it. You would only make payments on the money you use, similar to a credit card, and also have the ability to access that money again after you have paid off a portion of it. In this sense, a home-equity line of credit is not fixed but "revolving."

From an investment strategy standpoint, these are 2 great tools. We could lay out 100 different scenarios where 1 or the other is preferred. But I'll say it again: *it really comes down to your goals.* What are you trying to accomplish? This is where having your roadmap laid out is key. Are you trying to increase your cash flow or accumulate more assets?

Below is a side-by-side comparison of cash-out refinancing, home-equity lines of credit, and home equity loans, as well as their respective pros and cons.

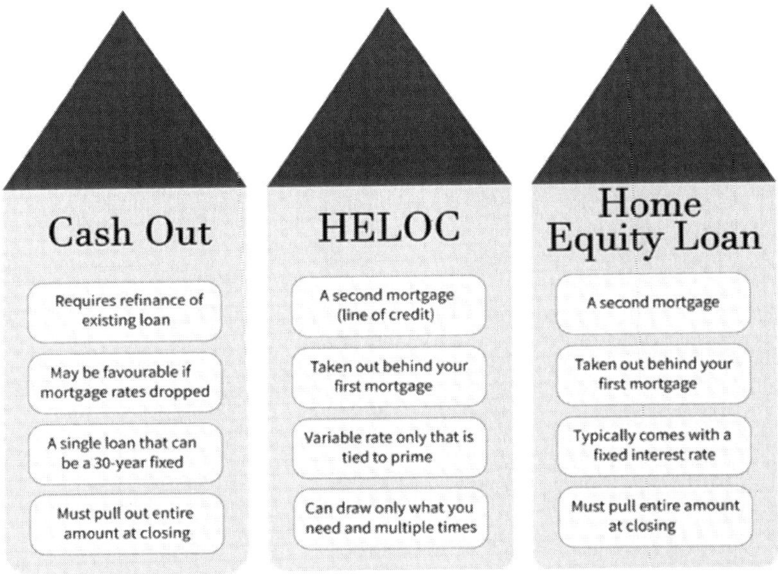

KEY POINTS

- Refinancing allows you to obtain a new loan with either a different interest rate or loan duration to help pay off the previous loan or borrow money off the full value of the property loan.
- A home equity loan allows you to refinance a portion of the full home value at a higher interest rate.
- A home equity line-of-credit is a second position mortgage that allows you to utilize the funds like a credit card.

SECRET 17

Finding the Right Deal is Simple Arithmetic

"A penny saved is a penny earned."

—Benjamin Franklin

Now that you understand how much money you could be earning through real estate investment; you are probably thinking: *What's a good deal look like? What's a great deal, and moreover, what's the worst deal I could make?* First, take a deep breath. When it comes to deal analysis, beginner investors tend to overthink. Analyzing a deal is not difficult though. Treat your investments like a business by breaking them down into income (profits) and expenses (losses). The income should exceed the expenses by a comfortable amount. With a greater margin between your income and expenses, the better your business is performing. How do you boost your business? Easy. Increase your income or reduce your expenses.

That's really it. If you can do simple addition and subtraction, you can analyze a deal.

Let's consider this hypothetical situation: You find a 3-family house listed for sale in a quaint neighborhood and want to know whether this would be a good purchase. Start by looking at the information you have about the property. In this case, 1 unit is vacant for you to move into and the other 2 occupied units each collect $1500 per month, for a total of $3000 per month in rent. There is also a coin-operated laundry onsite, which yields another $100 per month, for a total income of $3100 per month.

Remember cash flow? In that case, what would your expenses be? You'd have a mortgage payment, taxes, insurance, trash, water, and some utilities. When you add all these numbers together, assume it's a total of $2900 per month.

Now take your income and subtract your expenses to determine whether this deal is profitable. A quick calculation shows that you'd gain $200 in monthly profit ($3100 - $2900).

That's a pretty good outcome, but there is actually another bonus. In this example, you would basically live in 1 of the units for free because all of your expenses would be covered by your tenants' rent payments. If you assume that the market rate is exactly the $1500 that you're collecting per unit, you'd be saving that money by not paying your own rent, plus earning another $200 a month, for a total monthly profit of $1700.

What if your plans change, and in 1 year you decide to pack up and travel the world? If real estate prices are the same, you could rent your unit for $1500 like the other 2 in the building. At the same time that you'd be backpacking through Asia, you could be earning $4500 in rental income every month. What a nice pay out for truly very little effort!

But what about your expenses? With you off traveling, your tenants might ask you to hire a property management company for general upkeep. The company charges you 10% of gross rents, which is now $450 per month. Your original expense of $2900 per month increases by this amount, bringing your total expenses to $3350.

Overall, you still stand to gain a cash flow of $1250 monthly. Check out the math here: $4600 income (from rents + laundry) - $3350 expense (your original expense + property management cost) = $1250. All told, not a bad effort for a first-time investor.

Of course, the variables will change based on your particular situation, but I hope the lesson you learned is that deal analysis is plain simple arithmetic. Paralysis by analysis comes from fear of making the wrong move based on all the details of the deal. The secret to overcome this? Get a pencil and paper and crunch the numbers.

KEY POINTS

- Treat your investment like a business: the more your income exceeds the expenses, the better your business is performing.
- Tally up the potential income and expenses to figure out the right deal for you.
- Fight paralysis by analysis by focusing on the numbers.

SECRET 18

Being a Landlord isn't Difficult

"Don't tell me where your priorities are. Show me where you spend your money and I'll tell you what they are."

— James W. Frick

Maybe by now you have taken the plunge and bought your first multi-family as an investment property. Congratulations! Or you are still in the planning phase and want to understand all the responsibility you are signing up for. Either way, once you make the commitment to buy a rental property, you instantly become a landlord. This chapter of the book is about the lessons I have learned as a landlord, and I hope reading it will save you some stress and costs, both in time and money.

1. Do Your Research

Have a spare weekend or some time to kill? Then head to a home improvement store like Lowe's or Home Depot. Let's face it – your tenants won't all be angels, so if you want to maintain your own properties on a budget, scope out the costs of materials beforehand. Figure out what you're comfortable doing without the help of a contractor and what tools you might need to tackle the job.

Even perusing the aisles of a Home Depot can be valuable, if only to understand material costs. For example, if a plumber wants to charge you $600 to replace a toilet in 1of your units, would that be considered expensive? From your last trip to the store, you know that a standard toilet costs between $100 and $200. The plumber is essentially charging you $400 to $500 in labor. For a job that should take no more than an hour, I would say this is rather expensive. Personally, I would opt to get quotes from other plumbers or to replace the toilet myself and save even more money. Thinking longer term, the knowledge you gain by walking around the home supply stores and learning material costs will be useful should you ever decide to renovate.

What if you are short on time but still want to be a hands-on landlord? Then look no further than YouTube. There are millions of videos available on home maintenance projects that you can view from the convenience of your phone or laptop. You can search for any home improvement task and watch someone explain it step-by-step for free on YouTube. Of course, the quality of the content varies, but I've probably saved tens of thousands of dollars over the years from spending just a few minutes at a time watching these free tutorials. Even if you have no interest in doing the work personally or are unable to, I think it's worthwhile to watch these how-to videos to help you understand the time, effort, and skill involved in the job you want done.

2. Understand Your Legal Responsibilities

They say the road to hell is paved with good intentions, and this applies to being a landlord as well. As a landlord, you of course want to offer your tenants a clean, safe, accessible living situation, but what are you legally obliged to do to meet this end? You certainly don't need a law degree, but you do need to familiarize yourself with federal and local landlord tenant laws. A great resource is the wide selection of landlord-tenant related law books from NOLO. I like these books because they are easy to read and understand despite the complexity of the material. I recommend you keep them on your desk more as reference guides for when specific situations arise, but you could read them in their entirety if you wish.

As a landlord, it's your responsibility to understand the law regarding special populations. Federal legislation like the Americans with Disabilities Act (ADA) details certain building parameters that ensure accessibility rights for all your tenants. Be aware that there may also be local laws that address the needs of these and other groups. For instance, in Boston - a city founded in 1630 - the housing stock is much older compared to that of other metropolitan hubs in the country. The majority of our buildings were built before 1978 and therefore may contain lead paint. Lead paint negatively impacts child development, especially for those under the age of 6, and as a landlord in an older city, it would be your job to identify and minimize/eliminate this risk.

3. Create A Paper Trail

Keep good records. Whether they are mortgage documents, tenant files, rent receipts, or maintenance costs, anything associated with your business should be saved. In this case, once is good, but twice is extra nice. It's my way of saying keep paper files as well as (multiple) electronic backups of these documents. Create an organization system that works for you. That way you can quickly access these files in the future for whatever purpose e.g. tax preparation, protection against litigation, or even portfolio planning.

4. Take Your Emotions Out of the Equation

Surprisingly, managing tenants can be like parenting. There can be mood swings, tears, and rebellions, but your job is to stay levelheaded through it all. Similar to raising children, you should not hop on the emotional roller coaster with your tenants. As a landlord, you have to put your emotions aside, and lead with logic in every situation. Dealing with different tenant personalities is one of the most difficult aspects of property management, but like raising children, can be rewarding if you learn how to keep your feelings in check and strive for meaningful relationships with your tenants.

Remember that you're in business now, even if this is your first purchase and your primary residence. With all the income and expenses to consider, your rental property represents a major wealth-building opportunity, and ultimately emotions should not be a factor in your decision-making.

KEY POINTS

- Learn the costs of material goods so you understand what repairs and renovations should cost.
- Research landlord-tenant law, and apply what you learn.
- Leasing property is a business; maintain complete records of everything and check your emotions at the door.

MONEY SMARTS

How to Become an Expert:

The 10,000 Hour Rule:

Says it Takes 10,000 Hours Working on Your Craft or Niche to Hit Expert Level

That's Roughly 40 Hours per Week for 5 Years. Get to Work!

MONEY SMARTS

How Can I Make $1,000,000?

Sell a $200 Product to 5000 People
Sell a $500 Product to 2,000 People
Sell a $1000 Product to 1,000 People
Sell a $2000 Product to 500 People
Sell a $4000 Product to 250 People
Or
5000 People Pay $17/ Month, For 12 Months
2000 People Pay $42/ Month, For 12 Months
1000 People Pay $83/ Month, For 12 Months
500 People Pay $167/ Month, For 12 Months
250 People Pay $333/ Month, For 12 Months

SECRET 19

Pinpoint Your Real Estate Niche to Get Rich

"The successful warrior is the average man, with laser-like focus."

–Bruce Lee

Ever since I was a kid, unless it was basketball, I've had trouble staying focused on 1 particular thing for a long period of time. I often felt scatterbrained and disorganized, and in the beginning it greatly impacted my rental property business. I made many mistakes by not fully committing to certain opportunities and going after "shiny objects" instead. Over the years though, I've narrowed my focus and I try to teach new investors to do the same for themselves as early as possible. My business is laser-focused at this point. Specifically, I invest in rentals within 1 city, 1 property type, and 1 building type. Most of my industry peers would say that I'm super niche, and I can't argue with them. Rather, I like to say that I understand my product as an investor, and would recommend that you focus in the same way if you want to maximize your profits.

How do you find a niche for yourself then? While it may not work for every investor, I find that mapping out the following qualities helps me to better understand my "product," and thus make the best investment possible.

Geographic Niche

Not all rental property is created equal. Single-family rentals in Alabama don't move and operate the same as multi-family rentals in Detroit. At some point in your career as an investor, you must choose a geographic area, ideally 1 or 2 states, and really learn their ins and outs. Ask yourself: *What are the economic factors that affect rents there? Are large employers bringing new business to the area or shutting down for good?*

Get a sense of the politics. *Is it easy to build new developments, or are there countless restrictions and codes to abide?* Stay away from national news when it comes to making decisions on your rental properties. National trends aren't necessarily the same trends that are taking place in your niche markets. Markets in Kansas could be experiencing downturns while comparable markets in Florida are booming with low inventory. Moreover, there could be 2 side-by-side neighborhoods within South Florida with vast differences in how their markets perform.

Property Type

Knowing your property type is just as important as knowing your geographic niche. Property types consist of *residential* and *commercial.* The residential bracket can be further sub-divided into single-family and multi-family properties. Residential and commercial markets within the same city likely have different dynamics. For instance, if a massive casino is built in a particular neighborhood it may encourage more commercial business growth surrounding the facility. On the other hand, residential home prices may plummet as residents move away from the increased traffic. Savvy investors specialize in either residential or commercial property types, and understand how changes to a particular neighborhood can affect their property values, rent values, and investment longevity.

Whichever property type you choose, make sure that it makes sense within the market of your chosen geographic area. In the Northeast, it's difficult to find many neighborhoods where single-family properties will yield sufficient cash flow because rent prices for those are generally high compared to rental values. Thus, you would end up expending so much effort for such little cash flow potential if you opted to invest in single-family residences there. This is certainly not the case everywhere across the country, and it may be easy enough to reconsider your geographic niche depending on your investment goals.

Price Point

Develop your real estate niche even further by zeroing in on your ideal price point. Price points can vary widely within a specific neighborhood or city. *At what price point do you want to operate?* It is your job as an investor to understand values inside and out so that you can recognize good deals when they're presented to you. Price point also helps you determine rehab and repair budgets, and the value of those improvements. You don't want to overbuild or over improve for the target tenant or the neighborhood.

Tenant Base

Having a specific real estate niche can also factor in tenant selection. Assuming that you're doing the property management or tenant selection yourself, you should know who the ideal tenant is for your market, property type, and price point. Consider the following: *What qualities are you looking for in an applicant? Are you willing to settle if the applicant doesn't meet all the criteria? Are they market-based tenants or subsidized? Are your tenants also college or graduate students, and therefore likely to only rent for 9 months instead of 12 before returning home?*

Overall, the narrower your investment focus, the greater your ability to make sound financial decisions. Below is a list of reasons why identifying and locking in a specific real estate niche can maximize your wealth building efforts. Keep these in mind as you start on your real estate investment journey, and to help you ignore all the distractions and "shiny objects" that you may encounter.

1. You can knock out the competition and secure a great deal FASTER because you will require less time/effort for due diligence.
2. You can recognize trends within a neighborhood and make adjustments to your investment strategy ahead of the curve.
3. You understand labor cost and know what your job should be priced at.
4. You provide contractors, local vendors, and suppliers with repeat business and may therefore receive preferred pricing.
5. Wholesalers become familiar with your niche business model, and may be more willing to bring you deals before they hit the open market.
6. You understand the rental trends and your tenant base, and use this knowledge to maximize rental income in your units.
7. Lenders may feel more comfortable with your business when they realize that you understand the local markets.
8. You can tap into *economies of scale*, where having multiple rental properties can offer discounted pricing. For example, my snow removal guy would typically charge $100 per property, but because I have 3 locations, he gives me a discount of just $75 per property.

KEY POINTS

- Understand your niche, be it residential or commercial.
- Specialize in a certain type of property (such as single or multi-family homes within residential real estate) and understand the price points associated with these properties.
- Identify your ideal tenant and work to establish relationships with vendors and wholesalers in your geographic niche.

SECRET 20

Unit Count Doesn't Really Matter

"Quality is more important than quantity. One home run is much better than two doubles."

—Steve Jobs

In business, a product's value boils down to quantity vs quality. The same is also true in real estate investing. In my experience, people tend to focus on the wrong metrics when investing in real estate. To some investors, it seems impressive to be able to disclose the vast number of doors (rental units) that they own on a Podcast or in a networking meeting. The underlying assumption of course is that the more doors owned, the more talented and wealthier the investor. This is a false assumption, and we will get into the reasons why below. But before we move on, I need to emphasize again that your business plan is extremely important, and that you must review your goals on a regular basis. Your mission in successful real estate investment isn't about collecting doors - or at least it shouldn't be. *Your mission is about financial freedom.*

Suppose you have 2 investment colleagues, Ricky and Mike. Ricky owns 10 doors that produce roughly $1000 per door every month in cash flow. Ricky thus earns roughly $10,000 each month, or $120,000 annually. In comparison, Mike owns 100 doors, each producing about $100 per month in cash flow. Mike in essence also makes $10,000 per month, with the same yearly total.

By all accounts, Ricky and Mike appear to be performing equally well, despite Mike owning 10 times the number of rental units as Ricky. But what if we specify that Ricky increases rent on his 10 units by 5% per year, while Mike grows his rental income by only 3% per year? Furthermore, Ricky could have a 2% vacancy rate, while Mike's vacancy rate might be 8%.

With these new considerations, I would argue that Ricky is in the better financial position even though he owns 90 fewer units than Mike. Ricky objectively has a lower turnover rate, and raises his rents at a faster pace each year. His income will outpace Mike's in the very near future. Moreover, Ricky might have a better outlook on his investment because he may not be spread as thinly as Mike is in their respective property management responsibilities.

The moral of this example is to not get caught up in the hype when people start flexing their muscles about unit count. The acquisition of units is an exciting part of the journey, but it is not the destination. Ultimately, you should do what makes the most sense for you with regard to your goals, while realistically factoring in what you can accomplish or want to manage.

KEY POINTS

- The quality of your real estate investment can be far more profitable long-term than the quantity.

- Focus on your goals of wealth-building and financial freedom; avoid unit count envy.
- Understand the other factors that can help your investment grow, such as well-timed rent increases and tenant retention.

MONEY SMARTS

Real Estate Makes You Rich

You Can Take Control of Real Estate With Only a Small Percentage of the Purchase Price & Pay for Balance Over 30-40 Years.

This is Called: Leverage

MONEY SMARTS

Fortunes Are Made During Bad Economic Times by Those Who Focused on the Future.

Play the Long Game.

SECRET 21

There's No Need to Fear Uncle Sam

"Formal education will make you a living; self-education will make you a fortune."

— Jim Rohn

New real estate investors often feel overwhelmed by the prospect of filing taxes on their rental properties. It may seem that 1 wrong claim or a small clerical error could put a person in dire financial and legal straits, but I want to assure you that there is very little to fear. Just like with deal-finding (covered in Secret 17), the key to preventing tax-related disasters is as simple as another primary school topic: writing.

First and foremost, though, separate your personal banking from your rental business banking to stay organized throughout the tax year. As a new landlord, it's crucial that you open a separate checking account (and maybe a credit card) for your rental business. Deposit all your rental income into this business checking account and only pay for rental expenses from that account. This will allow you to easily identify rental expenses when the time comes to file. In this way, your monthly bank statements can serve as excellent reference tools from year to year, without the hassle of weeding out personal items.

Next, keep a handwritten or electronic expense journal, and use it throughout the year to help you or your accountant properly prepare your returns. Sample journal entries include explanations for unordinary expenses, miles traveled for your rental business, items you paid for with cash, and/or any miscellaneous purchases that pertain to your business. If you can't be bothered to jot these items down physically, then consider utilizing Quicken Rental Property Manager. This is a terrific tool for landlords to maintain their rental records, and with its user-friendly settings, can save precious time on detailed tasks like capturing expense records without manual data entry.

In addition to your handwritten notes, keep hard copies or electronic files for receipts, invoices and anything else that documents your purchases. If you own more than 1 rental property, you should separate these records by property and year as required by your schedule E (the federal tax form completed for rental property owners).

To tie it all together, establish and maintain a meticulous record-keeping system for your rental properties. In the event of an IRS audit, you'll want to be able to easily show that you were eligible to claim your deductions. As an added incentive, for every $100 in tax deductions, you may receive approximately $25 in tax savings (for taxpayers in the 25% bracket). And so, it's in your best interest to keep accurate records and deduct everything to which you are entitled. Nolo's - Every Landlords Tax Deduction Guide is a great resource for learning about tax deductions and the filing requirements of landlords. Additionally, this book is updated annually with the newest versions of laws and tax codes.

While the idea of filing taxes can be fearsome for new landlords, remember that you have worked hard to pursue your dream of financial freedom. Never forget to put in just as much effort to protect what you have earned from the hands of the IRS and Uncle Sam; start with the basics and write it all down.

KEY POINTS

- Separate your personal from your business banking to facilitate faster tax return filing each year.
- Keep a handwritten or electronic journal to accompany your receipts and other documents to create a clear record of all of your yearly expenses.
- Maintain meticulous record keeping for all of your properties, tracked according to your federal tax bracket.

SECRET 22

You Can Make Money in Any Market

"A funny thing happens in real estate. When it comes back, it comes back up like gangbusters."

— Barbara Corcoran

In my experience, finding a deal is 1 of the most exhilarating aspects of my job, especially when it seems like all the right factors and players magically aligned themselves for that opportunity. But what are the circumstances that can affect all of those moving parts from coming together? To understand this, you need to know about markets, and how money and deals flow into and out of them.

A *buyer's market* is 1 where there is more inventory available than there are buyers, and so the buyer will have the upper hand in terms of bargaining power. There may be 5 homes available for sale for every buyer who is looking to purchase in that particular market. The supply exceeds the demand. In a buyer's market, prices stabilize as sellers have no need to compete for buyers' attention. As a buyer, you have less competition and could move onto the next deal if the seller doesn't want to play ball.

The opposite is true in a *seller's market*. Here, there is more demand than there is supply. In terms of real estate, there'll be more buyers looking to purchase property than there is inventory on the market available for sale. If you have 10 buyers for every 1 house that becomes available for sale, then prices will be driven upward because buyers would compete with each other for a limited supply of housing. On the flip side, sellers can hold fast to pricing and terms that render them greater profits.

It's important to understand that markets are local and the state of markets are determined by local factors…mostly. As stated before, markets vary from state to state, and they can even vary within districts of a certain city.

The Money Supply

When the economy is thriving and people are doing well, money is easy to come by for the average investor. This is because in a good economy, the unemployment rate is typically low, wages are up, people have disposable income to spend, and money moves freely. During an economic upswing, banks feel comfortable about the future and tend to loosen lending restrictions. For example, required credit scores may go down, loan-to-value ratios may go up, and overall underwriting requirements get pushed to the side.

In a bad economy, people may lose their jobs, the unemployment rate climbs, businesses and consumers slow their spending, and money doesn't flow through the economy as easily. Lenders aren't as confident in the economic state and will tighten their lending guidelines. Depending on how bad the economic situation is, foreclosure rates may rise, as well as eviction rates, as people struggle to pay for their housing.

With that said, real estate doesn't work on a national scale. Real estate is local. You can have 1 state or city doing really poorly while there is another area of the country that is thriving. Certain events, like the 2020 coronavirus pandemic, impact the country as a whole, but the response and recovery times won't be uniform across the country.

Deal Flow

In a good economy, while money may be easy to come by, buying opportunities may not be as plentiful. Whether you know them or not, there are likely other people in your area looking to build wealth through real estate investment, and they are essentially your competition. The marketing and lead generation tactics that you used in a bad market may not get you any responses in good economic times. In a bad economy, you may need to pitch your investment opportunity to 5 times as many lenders to find the 1 that suits your needs. You'll have to work hard to find deals when times are good, and equally hard to find money when times are bad.

Regardless of the status of the economy, there is opportunity for money to be made. By understanding your local market and the factors that impact it, you can adjust your investment strategy, and ultimately come out ahead of your competitors.

KEY POINTS

- Buyers have the upper hand when there is more inventory than demand, and sellers have the advantage when there is more demand than supply.
- Money is easier to come by in good economic times, but buying opportunities are harder to find.
- Money can be made in any economic state, good or bad, but the conditions for making money changes, so you should learn to adjust your focus to maximize your wealth in either situation.

MONEY SMARTS

If You Live Until You're 75 Years Old

And You Sleep 8 Hours Per Day
And Work 8 Hours Per Day

You've Spent...
25 Years Sleeping
25 Years Working
25 Years Enjoying Life

Rentals Make Money While You Sleep So You Can Take More Time to Enjoy Life

MONEY SMARTS

Real Estate Makes You Rich

When You Buy Rental Real Estate, You Have Income & Expenses. When Your Income Exceeds Your Expenses, You're Putting Money in Your Pocket. This Is Called: Cash Flow

SECRET 23

Smart Landlords Love Section 8

"He who is not courageous enough to take risks will accomplish nothing in life."

— Muhammad Ali

If you're not familiar with the term *section 8*, it is a federal housing program for low income families, the disabled, and the elderly. Its purpose is to assist "voucher holders" in finding housing in the private market. The program is typically administered by local government (local housing authorities) and rent payments are paid directly to the landlord each month.

For those of you already familiar with this program, I imagine that it might evoke negative connotations. I'd like to expose a myth that exists in the rental property space. Specifically, that you should avoid owning section 8 eligible housing because those tenants will cause you more problems than market rate ones. When I first got into the business, I can honestly admit that I believed this stereotype. I heard horror stories from fellow real estate investors about voucher-based tenants creating unnecessary drama for landlords, and even destroying their rental properties. In hindsight, this was foolish and just plain wrong of me. I now know that a bad tenant is a bad tenant, regardless of how they are able to pay the rent. Today, 75% of my tenant base are voucher holders and I absolutely love it.

Many landlords incorrectly assume that section 8 tenants "play under a different set of rules." They believe that voucher holders have different application or acceptance processes than persons who do not qualify for the subsidy. *This is only true if you choose to make it that way*. As a landlord, you should have clear-cut, unbiased standards for your future tenants.

Below is an example set of criteria that applicants should meet in order to be considered as tenants for your apartments:

- A minimum credit score of 650
- Income and employment verification
- No smoking and/or no pets
- Criminal background check
- Four months' rent as security deposit
- Last month's rent

Of course, you should first verify that these requirements don't violate your state or local laws prior to accepting applications, but my point is that you should establish minimum qualifying standards for your tenants. In this way, voucher holding applicants wouldn't get a pass from meeting these standards due to their status since these don't pertain to that. As long as your application requirements don't vary from 1 person to the next (which is a form of discrimination), you can ensure that you have high-quality tenants by creating and upholding objective criteria.

Some people might argue that the standards listed above are still too stringent or even perhaps biased. Section 8 voucher holders typically have 70 to 100% of their rent paid by the subsidy, so why would I ask for income verification? That's a fair question. My response would be to consider the other things that that tenant would be responsible for paying. These include utilities, food, transportation, clothing, household goods, and anything else that they would need to live safely if not comfortably. Renting to someone with a voucher who then can't pay for heating or cooling can be very risky and, in some situations, dangerous. They could potentially damage your unit by letting the pipes freeze in the winter if they can't afford to pay for the utilities, and in hot weather, could endanger their own health if they don't want to use the cooling system. In this sense, knowing that your tenants are voucher based can help you identify potential pitfalls and be more transparent about your selection process.

An advantage of renting to voucher based tenants is that their vouchers are income-dependent. If they lose their job or their hours are reduced at work, they can then request to have their subsidies adjusted accordingly by their caseworker. This is especially useful in a bad economy where droves of people are laid off unexpectedly, or in extreme cases like the COVID-19 pandemic where people may not be allowed to work outside of their homes for public safety reasons. In hard economic times, voucher-heavy landlords are better able to weather these changes as long as the local government or voucher provider continues to pay the tenants' bills.

On the whole, it's pretty evident why I and other landlords view the section 8 program as a tremendous wealth-building and social opportunity. As a landlord to a large voucher-holding tenant base, I am still able to maintain high standards for my lessees, while being fair and unbiased. I can also withstand potential economic disasters better as I know that my income stream will likely be unaffected, as long as the local government continues to pay and adjust my tenants' subsidies. Finally, I can do a small part in reducing the stigma that my tenants may experience by later providing a strong reference for them should they choose to move to other private housing.

You can find out more about the section 8 programs at:

https://www.hud.gov/topics/housing_choice_voucher_program_section_8

Check your local public housing authority for specifics in your market.

KEY POINTS

- Section 8 is a federal housing program that subsidizes rent for certain groups of disadvantaged people.
- Accepting voucher-based tenants offers many advantages, including a more secure rental income stream during times of economic uncertainty.
- Create fair, unbiased, and high-quality standards that apply to all of your tenants.

Section 4

Stack Your Odds With Good Teammates

SECRET 24

Never Stop Feeding Your Funnel

"I will tell you how to become rich. Close the doors. Be fearful when others are greedy. Be greedy when others are fearful."

—Warren Buffett

If you really want to be successful at real estate investing and scale faster, you need to find great deals. Not average or borderline deals, but really great deals. Most investors find their first property through a real estate agent or by searching the Multiple Listing Service (MLS), but this process won't work if your goal is to build a massive portfolio because everyone has access to the Internet and to MLS. Simple economics predicts that this is a near-impossible way to find great deals; a limited supply of suitable investment housing coupled with a vast number of investors will likely drive prices upward. When the price goes up, your chance at a great deal vanishes.

So how do you find properties that will really help you scale without the hassle of competing with countless other buyers? *Pre-market* and *off-market properties.* Pre-market properties are listings that come to your attention before they are posted to MLS. This is oftentimes a property that you might've heard about through your real estate connections, and now have the jump on prior to it being made public knowledge.

An off-market property is any potential piece of real estate sold by an agent who is not using the MLS. Occasionally, listing brokers will find that selling a property quietly is the best course of action for all parties involved. The 2 major reasons why they might opt for this are: 1) the seller wishes to avoid drawing attention to the sale and potentially disturbing the current inhabitants, or 2) the seller wants to deter window shoppers. In the former case, the seller or landlord may not want to impose on the tenants' space with large open houses, yard signs, or public photos of the property (that may include the tenant's possessions). In the latter, the seller may want to weed out non-serious buyers and focus only on tenable offers.

As a side-note, when I say multi-family, I am referring to any property consisting of 2 to 4 separate units. This would be considered residential property, whereas any property with 5 or more units is technically a commercial investment property, and thus has a different set of rules and considerations to be successfully managed. For the purpose of this book, I will only be referring to 2- to 4- unit residential properties when discussing multi-family investing, as they are what I deal in everyday and have built my own wealth around.

In my experience, anything with 5 units or more tends to have savvy owners and deal-minded brokers. It is rare to find a below-market or great deal with these players because of how experienced and specialized they are. On the other hand, I find that the odds are more in your favor in the residential multi-family space because there may be distressed properties or distressed owners willing to sell at discounted or under-market prices. Personally, If I am looking to buy rent-ready properties, I target ones with values that are "80 cents to the dollar." In other words, I only want to spend $80,000 for every $100,000 that the property is worth. With this strategy, my net worth immediately grows as soon as I sign on the dotted line at the closing table because I've bought an asset that's worth more than the debt or liability that's attached to that asset.

Taking a step back though, let's think about why anyone would want to sell for less than market value.

1. Bad economy. If the stock market performs poorly, people tend to make rash decisions because they may worry about losing their jobs or income. If they want to sell in this particular time, they may need to undercut the market. Going back to basics, in a bad economy, there may be more houses for sale on the market than potential buyers. The majority of people will be scared, and view this as a terrible time to acquire property. You however after reading this book, will understand that when these people move left, you should be looking for opportunities on the right. If you're 1 of the only buyers and there are several people who are looking to sell in this market, then you now have the bargaining power to make the best deal.

2. Distressed property. The definition of a distressed property actually hinges on a few factors, including the physical condition of the property, and the personal and financial stability of the owner. Properties become distressed in good or bad markets. A physically distressed house is 1 that is in really bad condition. It has fallen into a state of disrepair for whatever reason, such as a sick or elderly owner who can't keep up with maintenance. Or, the house may have been willed to the owner's kids, who in turn have zero interest in their inheritance. Regardless, a physically distressed home is an excellent way to buy property at an extreme discount. The seller may not want to risk any liability by holding open houses and having potential buyers walk through a messy, unsafe property. They may simply be ashamed of the house's appearance, and would like to sell it quickly and quietly to an investor. That investor could be you if you can look beyond the physical condition of the property, and see the potential wealth it could offer once you renovate it.

3. Distressed seller. In this situation, there may not be anything wrong with the property itself, but the seller must sell the property quickly and is willing to accept less money for it. Personally, distressed sellers may be reacting to sudden divorce, injury/illness, or a death in the family.

I want to emphasize that the goal of real estate investing is not to take advantage of another person's misfortune. While divorce, illness, or death can befall anyone and now occur more frequently in the setting of a rapidly expanding elderly population, responsible real estate investors don't capitalize on someone else's hardships and make a bad circumstance worse. The goal is to create a win-win situation for both parties. You should never force someone to sell or feed them false information to sway their decisions. Instead, offer these distressed sellers reasonable solutions to their present problems, and respect their decisions if they decline your offer.

Overall, as a smart real estate investor, you should ideally buy property under market value to achieve your great deal. This will allow you to walk in and have equity from day 1. Tap into your network to find pre- or off-market deals, zig when others zag in uncertain economic times, and if possible, look for distressed properties or sales that will keep more money in your pocket.

KEY POINTS

- Some of the best deals can be found in pre-market or off-market deals.
- You may be able to find under-market value homes during bad economic times.
- You also may be able to find sellers with distressed properties or situations in which they will sell below market value.

SECRET 25

Success Comes From Who, Not What

"Landlords grow rich in their sleep."

—John Stuart Mill

"Your network is your net worth."

This is one of the most clichéd sayings in business, but it's the truth. Aligning myself with people who think like me and seek to achieve the same things in life was 1 of the smartest things I've ever done. My network and business connections have made or saved me hundreds of thousands of dollars. While I take pride in my formal education, I've realized that I can only learn so much from books, especially in a world that's constantly changing. And so I surround myself with people who are also pursuing financial education, and I learn from them. They teach me about their strategies and best practices, and in return, I share my experiences and we consistently offer supportive feedback.

In 2012, I stumbled upon what came to be 1 of the most rewarding aspects of my career: Meetup.com. At the time, I was feeling unfulfilled in terms of my financial aspirations, and isolated because I didn't have anyone with whom to discuss these goals. I've always had a core group of friends, but our ambitions didn't necessarily match. After seeing the power of the Meetup.com platform, I decided to start my own group called Boston Wealth Builders. Today, BWB has well over 2000 members, and I've met some incredible people through this network. Even if you don't want to create a new group, I would encourage you to check out sites like Meetup, EventBrite, or any other networking platform you can to find that group of people who share your same goals and interests.

The people you surround yourself with may ultimately make or break your financial future. I believe that we are ultimately the products of our environment, but that we each have the ability to create or dictate those environments. Find the people who are trying to do what you want to do or who have already done it, and learn what you can from each other.

Suppose these like-minded individuals are few and far between. What then could you do in order to work on your growth mindset? Or put in a different way, would you spend $50 to learn how to make $50,000? One thing that I encourage all of my mentees to do is keep a budget of $50 to $100 that is earmarked for growing their network. Use the money for lunch. Really. Or dinner if you prefer. What I mean is that when you're networking and meeting people, you'll find someone that you truly admire. I want you to reach out to that person (or people) at least once a month, and offer to take them to lunch or dinner. You can then use that meal as an opportunity to practice "informational interviewing," and pick apart the specifics of what drives their success.

You might be thinking that my advice is best suited for young, idealistic people who don't have any responsibilities to worry about. Or you might be thinking that there is no way the person you want for your mentor would even have the time of day for you. I want you to put all of that anxiety aside for a moment and think about the opportunity cost of the situation. (See Secret 13 for a refresher on this concept.)

Let's say you call up a potential mentor and she is only able to meet you on a Tuesday for lunch. She spends nights and weekends with her family, and of course conducts her business during the week. But what if you work a similar schedule? To figure out your opportunity cost in this situation, suppose you make roughly $50,000 per year or $200 per day. If taking a day off of work will cost you $200 in wages plus $50 in lunch, you have now invested $250 to potentially learn something or make a connection that could yield you $50,000-100,000 in investing or business tips. When laid out in these terms, the choice is obvious.

Once you establish connections with your mentors and peers, remember to always act in a manner that protects your reputation.

In reality, we live in a small world within smaller cities, that have tiny industries within those. The real movers and shakers all know each other. I've observed a lot of people who could've been incredibly successful suddenly become *persona non grata* because they didn't protect their reputations. They try to make big gains by taking advantage of others. Don't stoop to that. Don't burn bridges. Do everything you can to "keep your nose clean." Pay people what they are due and pay them on time. Be an upstanding citizen and your network will explode. People who don't try to take shortcuts are rare, and in return, others will take notice in a good way.

From your network you'll also be able to assemble and maintain a great team of professionals. Ask your network to connect you with a good CPA, bookkeeper, attorney, financial advisor, insurance provider, business lender, and mortgage broker. Get recommendations from the best of the best. The wealthy don't settle for "just okay." Remember that the best advice will cost you hundreds while saving you thousands.

My network today is 1 of my greatest business assets. It's hard to put a quantitative value on having the ability to call or email a group of smart, driven people and immediately receive answers to your pressing questions. Good networking will bring you into deals and opportunities not available to the general public. Private placements, real estate syndications, and business start-ups are not available to everyone, so leverage your willingness to learn and your good name to get your foot in the door. This is how the rich get richer.

KEY POINTS

- The cliché is true - your network is your net worth.
- Join a networking group or start one yourself.
- Keep a small amount of money in your weekly budget to allow for networking with outstanding individuals.

MONEY SMARTS

Most of Us Spend More Money on the Weekends While Not Working Than We Do During the Week. When You Retire, Isn't Everyday a Weekend?

Start Planning Now

MONEY SMARTS

Real Estate Makes You Rich

Over Time Real estate tends to increase in value as the supply is limited and demand for housing continues to grow with our population growth. This Is Called: Appreciation

SECRET 26

Good Lenders Are Bespoke

"You miss 100% of the shots you don't take."

— Wayne Gretzky

So far, we have discussed the why and when of real estate investment, but let's dive a little deeper into the how. For most people, the how involves finding a mortgage broker to help you get pre-approved for a loan. This is a critical crossroads where so many would-be investors make the wrong move and their real estate journey ends as quickly as it begins. Here are 4 pieces of advice to help you avoid this failure, and come out on top of the mortgage process.

1. Stay away from the national banks

Too many investors head to the same lending institution where they have their checking account when they go searching for loans. The big national banks can be great for establishing checking, savings, and credit cards accounts, but aren't typically the best place to find your mortgage. Think about it this way: shopping for a mortgage at a big national bank is like shopping for a suit at JC Penney's, Macy's, or Sears. You will certainly find suits there, but you'll be limited in terms of size, color, and other customizations. You might find something to wear, but it may not fit you and your exact needs.

What you really want is a local community bank in the neighborhood where you're looking to buy property, and thus a local mortgage broker. If you're able to tell the mortgage broker what you're looking for, it's like getting your suit tailor-made. The focus is on you, and you no longer feel like you're shopping at a big box store. Mortgage brokers have access to many different loan programs and with their help, you increase your chances of avoiding cookie-cutter mortgages. Also, if you've been denied by the big banks in the past, it doesn't mean that you won't ever qualify for a home loan. It could simply mean that you didn't fit into one of the suits that they had on the rack.

2. Don't be just another number

In the eyes of the big national brands, your wants and needs mean very little. You are Loan Application #56924 and not much more. Another reason to use a local mortgage broker is the personal relationship that you could build with them. Real estate can be a fast-moving business, especially in a seller's market, and you need to have an open line of communication with your mortgage broker. With national chains, you are constrained by their schedule, usually Monday through Friday, 9AM to 5PM. This wouldn't bode well if you had questions that needed answering outside of that timeframe. And so I prefer to work with mortgage brokers who are available via cell phone outside of banking hours, and who moreover are genuinely interested in helping me. In real estate, the best deals don't abide by the Monday-Friday, 9 to 5 work schema. They can happen late-night or on the weekends, and if you need a slight adjustment or have a question about your pre-approval, you need to have ready access to a knowledgeable, live person.

3. Your mortgage broker isn't doing you a favor

So many of my clients are afraid to call mortgage brokers and lenders to ask questions about their pre-approval prospects. I think the fear stems from the concern that these finance professionals are super busy and hate to have their time wasted. Of course you don't want to do that either, but you also deserve to have your questions answered by an informed expert. The mortgage broker isn't doing you a favor by answering your questions; it is part of his or her job. If someone doesn't treat you with respect, move on to the next broker and find someone who does. Your mortgage broker should also understand that you're an investor and plan to buy multiple properties. Multiple properties in most cases means multiple loans and thus multiple opportunities to get paid by working with you.

4. Rental income helps you qualify for more

So many new investors talk to the bank or mortgage broker and simply state that they want to be pre-approved. They provide the documentation the lender is asking for and receive their pre-approval letter. In some cases, they find out that the pre-approval is not enough to buy property in the town or city in which they want to live/invest. This is generally because what they got from the bank was a single-family pre-approval. The bank assumed that they were buying a single-family primary residence, and so the pre-approval was based on the investor's work income only. This neglects the rental income that the investor would receive after buying the multi-family property, which is a shame because this figure would increase the pre-approval spending limit. Let's take a look at the example below to explore how this would work:

Single Family Home Purchase Pre-Approval	4-Family Home Purchase Pre-Approval
Your work income = $30,000	Your work income = $30,000 Your potential rental income = $18,000 [You live in 1 unit and rent the other 3 out for $500 per month. $1500 a month times 12 months is $18,000 per year.] Work income + rental income = $48,000
Your single-family pre-approval =$200,000	Your multi-family pre-approval number = $375,000

You now qualify for a greater loan simply by adding in the assumed rental income after purchase. Ideally, you and your mortgage broker should consider 4 different pre-approval scenarios: a single-family, 2-family, 3-family, and 4-family pre-approval. The mortgage broker will need to "assume" or estimate rents for the multi-family pre-approvals, and make adjustments when necessary depending on the actual rental income of your potential property. This is where an open line of communication with your mortgage broker is key, because it allows for quick changes to your pre-approval letter that ultimately gives you a leg up on competing offers to the seller.

KEY POINTS

- Choose to work with local community banks and mortgage brokers over national chains to get insight and prospects customized to your needs.
- Don't be afraid to ask questions of your mortgage broker. Establish a personal connection to allow for a flexible working relationship.
- Remember to factor in your potential rental income when applying for a pre-approved loan on your multi-family property.

SECRET 27

Going Solo Can Actually Work in Your Favor

"Owning a home is a keystone of wealth, both financial affluence and emotional security."

— Suze Orman

The other day I was sitting in the waiting room at my dentist's office when I happened to glance at the TV. It was muted but on screen, the camera had zoomed in on a young couple who seemed to be receiving the keys to what I gathered was their first home. They were ecstatic, and the consultants made the entire process look so easy. Then I remembered that not everything is what it appears to be on the TV screen.

To understand what I mean, we need to first unpack the concept of *debt-to-income ratio*, or DTI.

Your debt-to-income ratio is simply your monthly obligations (bills reported to the credit bureau) divided by your gross monthly income. Your reported debts would include payments on your car, house, credit cards, school loans, and any other monthly payments that are reported to the 3 credit bureaus. You may also have bills for your phone, Internet service, cable, and gym membership, however these obligations are likely not reported to the credit bureau. The average person's monthly obligation might look like this:

Car payment	$300
Credit card bill	$200
Student loan	$200
Total Obligation	**$700**

If your gross income was $2000 per month, then you would divide $700 by $2000 and end up with 0.35 or a 35% debt-to-income ratio.

In most cases, a 35% debt-to-income ratio is pretty good. But it becomes a little more complicated when you decide to purchase a home because most home loan lenders will not let a borrower exceed a DTI ratio of more than 50%.

Using the same figures from above, you therefore couldn't exceed $1000 in monthly payments of your $2000 total income should you wish to buy a home. In another sense, you would have roughly $300 to spend on a new mortgage, taxes, and insurance before you would meet the 50% debt-to-income ratio limit set by the lender. Realistically speaking, that would be extremely tight, and you wouldn't have many options for homes to purchase that fit those parameters. Your mortgage broker might suggest that you pay off a credit card, or possibly your student loan, to reduce your debt-to-income ratio.

Overall, your DTI ratio is a big factor when buying a home and especially when trying to invest in multiple homes. How then can the average person solve the DTI problem and secure more lending for themselves?

First, you and your spouse don't need to both be on the mortgage to own the house. Unlike the dreams that are sold on popular television like the 1 that I described at the beginning of this chapter, home ownership comes down to the mortgage, which ultimately depends on the buyer's(s') credit scores. It can be a good feeling for a young couple to buy a house together, but thinking more long-term, they may have provided the bank more information than needed. If 1 partner has the credit and income to secure the mortgage, it would be the better financial move to just have that person apply for the loan and close on the house. This leaves the other partner free of that monthly housing payment, keeping his or her DTI ratio low. Conversely, the bank would prefer to have both partners tied to the mortgage because it puts them in a better financial position. The loan is more secure with 2 people obligated to pay it. Understanding that only 1 person needs to be listed on the loan can create leverage against future lenders for the couple as a whole.

Second, the people named on the mortgage and on the deed don't necessarily have to be the same. A mortgage is a document that you provide to the bank stating that you will agree to pay the loan under the proposed terms. People often say, "I'm going to get a mortgage," but, in reality, you're giving the bank a mortgage on the property that you own. They are giving you a loan to purchase the property from the existing owner. The previous owner separately gives you a deed which shows that the ownership of the property has been transferred to you.

How does this help you? Let's say you and your spouse decide you want another property in the near future, and don't want both of you to be tied down with the same housing payment. You choose to go on the mortgage by yourself, and the bank agrees that you can afford to do so. After closing, you now own the house, have a new mortgage in your name, and the deed was recorded at your local registry. You can then add your spouse's name as an owner on the new deed. The 2 of you own the property together, but only 1 of you has the mortgage affecting that individual's DTI ratio. This could free up the other spouse's finances for future purchases. Before you put this into action however, speak to a local attorney who specializes in real estate about this strategy to ensure that it's legal in your state.

Continuing with the same scenario, imagine that a few years later, you and your spouse have some financial problems because you lost your job. It's only a temporary blip though and you're back to work within a few months. During that time, you were late with the mortgage payments. When this happens, your credit score gets "dinged." This is a red mark on your credit report that can stick around for several years and can hurt your chances of getting future loans. If both you and your spouse were tied to the mortgage, then the red flag would appear on both credit reports. But if only one of you were on the mortgage (and both on the deed), the ding would only affect one spouse, leaving the other's credit unscathed.

In *Business Secrets*, we will take this strategy a step further by getting everything out of your name (freeing up your DTI ratio), using an LLC, and having a separate tax identification number.

KEY POINTS

- The debt-to-income ratio is your monthly debts divided by your monthly income.
- When it comes to home loans, lenders prefer a lower range DTI, which can leave little wiggle room in your spending limits.
- When acquiring a mortgage with a spouse, check with local attorneys to see if your state allows you to leave 1 of your names off the mortgage (but still on the deed). This will help insulate your separate credit scores for future property purchases.

MONEY SMARTS

Most People Stop Reading After Graduation.

Don't Be Like Most People.

1 Book per Month =
12 Books per Year =
60 Books in 5 Years

You Can Gain a Wealth of Knowledge in 5 Short Years

MONEY SMARTS

Real Estate Makes You Rich

When You Own Rental Real Estate, Your Tenants Help You Pay Off Your Mortgage. With Each Monthly Mortgage Payment, You're Reducing Your Debt & Increasing Your Net Worth.

This is Called: Amortization

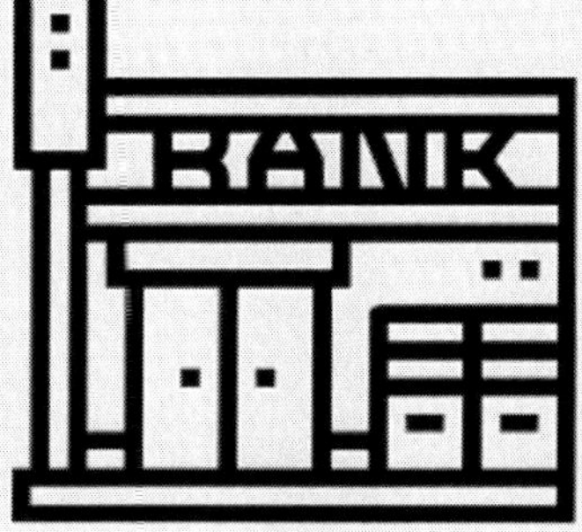

SECRET 28

Good Defense Now Can Mean Great Offense Later

"You want to know what a man is really like, take notice of how he acts when he loses money."

— Simone Weil

In Secret 9, I introduced you to the importance of credit, namely having a good score. When things aren't going well for you financially, you should look to protect your credit while paying off what you can if you've got debt accumulation. Credit can be the difference between being able to purchase a new home or not. Ultimately, a good credit score represents leverage when making financial decisions, and the higher the score, the more say you have in your purchases or applications.

To increase your credit score and your investment possibilities, make sure you're paying reported obligations on time. We discussed examples of these in Secret 27, i.e. car payments, mortgages, credit card bills, and student loan payments. If you can't determine whether to pay off your credit card bill or your Internet/cell phone bill, a good rule of thumb is to forego the inessential things that won't impact your record. It may be inconvenient to go without a cell phone for a little while, but it will be so insignificant in comparison when you can finally pay off your credit card debt.

Wherever you are in your journey to achieving good credit, always have enough money to pay for your reported obligations. This could mean reserving "rainy day funds," making meals at home vs. dining out, or doing more for yourself rather than paying others to do so. Calculate your ideal target for those funds by creating family and individual budgets. Go a step further and save up a "disaster cushion." If you're spending $4,000 a month, save at least $12,000-$16,000, or 3 to 4 months' worth of payments, in the event that something unpredictable happens and puts you out of work. Stash this money away first, and think long and hard before you make any discretionary purchases.

How to Never Be Denied for a Loan

On the subject of leverage, let's talk about the secrets to never being denied for a loan.

Banks are in the business of making money. Therefore, when banks give out loans, they expect you to pay the loan back with interest, which in turn generates profit for the bank. When applying for a loan, put yourself in the bank's shoes: *Would you give yourself the loan?* Are you (and your finances) reliable enough to profit the bank?

Banks consider 5 metrics when reviewing your loan application, and I like to refer to them as the **5 C's.**

The 5 C's are: Credit history, Capacity, Collateral, Capital, and Conditions.

For Credit history, the bank essentially checks whether or not you've paid your current bills on time. This is a good predictor for them that you will also be able to pay your loan on time and for the full amount.

Capacity refers to your financial ability to withstand the additional debt of the loan. They are also interested in determining whether you can pay them back with interest.

For the third C, Collateral, the bank examines what you already own that could be viewed as assets. This can be a number of things, from houses to cars to stocks and bonds. The more collateral you have, the more assurance the bank has that you have some other way to repay the loan should your income or revenue suddenly dry up.

In terms of Capital, the bank assesses what you have independently saved to date to make your purchase. While it is understood that you are applying for a loan from the bank to buy your property of interest, your transaction is technically a partnership, and thus they want to be sure that you will contribute meaningfully towards the end goal.

Finally, the term Conditions describes the bank's evaluation of what you plan to do with the money. If your purpose is clear and not something frivolous like a new flat-screen TV, then the bank will have confidence in your intentions, and fewer qualms about loaning you money.

The road to financial freedom can be confusing and almost hostile if you don't have a good roadmap, and I would say that the 5 C's are among those key tools to keep in your pocket to help you achieve your goals. I hope that by laying these out for you whole sum, it allows you to better examine your own financial situation and adjust your habits for greater success. Start small, and don't stop until you truly measure up.

KEY POINTS

- If you find yourself in a financial hardship, protect your credit above all else because it will be your ticket to financial freedom.
- Pay down reported obligations like credit card debt over other bills to maintain your leverage when applying for loans or making purchases.
- Become the ideal loan applicant by analyzing your finances in terms of the 5 C's, and make the necessary adjustments to become more worthy in the eyes of the banks.

Section 5

Take It All In

SECRET 29

A Real Estate License is a Gift and a Curse

"It is not that we have too little time to do all the things we need to do; it is that we feel the need to do too many things in the time we have."

— Gary Keller

I get asked fairly frequently about the ins and outs of wealth-building through real estate investment, and 1 question that comes up almost every time is whether a person should become a real estate agent first. In my opinion, you don't necessarily need a real estate license to be successful as an investor, but having 1 can help in certain situations. As with any major decision, you should weigh the pros and cons (opportunity cost) of obtaining your license. Here are a few considerations to help you come to the best decision for you.

In order to become licensed, you will need to take a class, study for the certifying exam, and eventually sit for the test. During that same time though, you could be doing other things to find investing opportunities. While some of the education you receive will assist you, a good portion of it will cover laws and procedures that won't necessarily apply to your investing endeavors.

If you do get your license, access to your local MLS can really help your investing. Housing ownership records are public information and are usually kept on the local county's Registry of Deeds. You can typically go to the county's website and plug in the owner's name or address to pull up records for that property. But with access to MLS as an agent, you typically have a more consolidated version of this that encompasses all of a state's counties in 1 central database. This is a powerful tool. By simply entering in an owner's name or address, you can find out the last sale, purchase price, mortgage information, prior owners, square footage, lot size, and an obscene amount of other useful data for that property. In turn, you can then quickly determine property values, rent values, days-on-market, and other vital information, and make quality investment decisions as a result. Lastly, you can also sift through photos of old listings on MLS or Zillow to help you determine the quality expectation of the local tenant base.

It goes without saying that time is of the essence when placing an offer to purchase a property. If you find an incredible deal on MLS, there are likely other investors also looking at that opportunity. Understanding what paperwork is necessary and how to complete an offer to purchase gives you a leg up on the competition. You're no longer waiting on your agent, but instead can submit your offer directly to the selling agent of the property you want. Negotiations can also be sped up by working directly with the selling agent.

A downside of having a license pertains more to the transaction aspect. As a real estate agent, when talking to a potential seller directly, you have to disclose that you are a licensed agent. As a salesperson, you are considered a "person of knowledge." This "superior" position needs to be disclosed in a situation where you are negotiating with a seller of a potential property you want to buy. It also needs to be disclosed when you go to sell any property you own. The person on the other end of the deal must be aware that they are interacting with someone experienced in the business; this can sometimes raise red flags to the other party. With that being said, you should never conceal that you hold a real estate license because you want to maintain a reputation of integrity.

Stay Neutral

Many investors become sale agents because they want to save money on sales commissions. They figure, if they get their license, they can buy and sell their own properties and won't need to pay a real estate agent for the work. While this is admirable, I would caution these individuals about having this outlook.

Specifically, because buying and selling real estate can be an emotional process, especially for your first few deals. Your first property may be one that you actually live in, and so you have an emotional pull towards the building. Most of us don't realize that that emotional connection exists until we try to sell the house and someone else verbally rips it apart. During a home inspection, a potential buyer can be brutal, criticizing everything that you felt was good about the property. Many times, the buyer is doing this as a negotiating tactic, but as a seller, it's still hard to receive criticism and negotiate from a place of logic. This isn't much different from when you're buying your first couple of properties.

With your first 2 or 3 purchases and/or sales, I would highly recommend using an experienced real estate salesperson to assist you, even if you have your license. To this day, I try to restrict as much contact as possible between myself and the buyer/seller on the opposite side. As I've said before, no matter how much we believe the opposite, humans are emotional beings and aren't always logical in our thinking. In my experience, the more time that a buyer and seller spend in the same space together, the more likely the deal is to fall apart.

Be Smart with Your Time – Rentals

As opposed to purchasing and sales, I argue that new investors should lease the first few units themselves to gain experience. If you enjoy doing it, then you can continue with that task. This is where having a real estate license is useful because you will be familiar with local tenant and landlord laws, and can avoid legal snafus when looking for applicants. But in the long run, I predict that you'll find that the leasing process isn't a good use of your time and perhaps more of a headache than what it's worth. If or when you decide to hand over the leasing process to another agent, you will free up more time for yourself. A good leasing agent will help you photograph and market the property to potential tenants. Your leasing agent can do the showings, and not only accept any applications but run necessary background checks and vet the applicants against your specific criteria. Leasing agents can also help with drafting documents such as a fully executed lease agreement. In the grand scheme of things, there's a lot of work that goes into correctly on-boarding a new tenant. You have enough to do as the owner, landlord, and investor, so it is nice to be able to offload some of the minutiae.

KEY POINTS

- Getting a real estate license can sharpen your investment advantage by granting you access to the MLS and its vast data.
- Being your own property's agent can stir up emotions and complicate face-to-face negotiations with potential buyers.
- Hiring a leasing agent frees up valuable time on your end, so find a good leasing agent who will work to accomplish these tasks to your standards and specifications.

SECRET 30

In It to Win It

"Marriage is a partnership, and couples can't win with money unless they budget as a team."

— Dave Ramsey

I find that a common issue that my clients regularly struggle with is convincing their significant others to get onboard with the path to wealth. There can be serious sacrifices and lifestyle changes that need to be made in order to achieve financial freedom, and not everybody can adjust so easily. It can be extremely challenging to be in a relationship where both partners view money and spending differently. I often feel like a marriage counselor when I coach my clients in having these deep conversations about their financial goals.

On one such occasion, a client of mine told me that he didn't feel the need to involve his spouse in this process, and that he was willing to take the journey alone. I was shocked at first, but after we discussed the topic a little further, I understood that he just didn't think she would buy in to his plan or methods. I should stress that putting your wealth building strategy into action without your partner's support is almost impossible to do. While you may be comfortable practicing moderation and only spending money when necessary, your spouse may not be, and this can derail your plans for the future for the both of you.

Take a moment to sit down with your partner and fully examine your family budget. Perhaps you could designate 1 of you as the financial point person in your relationship. Together, figure out how much money is coming in, how consistent this is, what expenses are going out, how to control and/or minimize them, (what) are you investing, and what happens if financial trouble comes. The answers to these questions most likely hinge upon your loved one's finances as well, and as such he or she has an equal stake in where your household's money goes.

With that said, I don't believe in combining everything when it comes to financials. My wife and I are on the same page with regard to our ultimate goals, but we still maintain separate personal credit cards and checking accounts. This serves to provide us with both privacy and personal accountability. At the end of the day, we are individuals and we trust each other enough to stay out of the other's spending. The way my wife and I manage our finances won't work for everyone, but regardless of what you are currently doing, you need to at least be open to and prepared for having these discussions.

I've only been married once, so I can't speak from experience, but the divorced people with whom I've interacted indicate that a lack of consistent communication was the downfall of their marriages, especially when it came to financial matters. Moreover, there was usually more than just a single opportunity to discuss these topics, since life kept unfolding with or without their say. So if you tried once to have the conversation and it didn't work out, try it again – the circumstances might have changed and your partner could be more receptive to what you have to share.

The following are examples of situation-dependent concerns regarding your finances that you should explore with your partner:

- What happens if one of us loses a job or income source?
- Do we have enough liquidity to make it through an economic slowdown?
- Will we have to support anyone besides ourselves, like elderly parents who are about to retire or (more) children?
- Are we paying for our children's college educations?
- What are the absolute necessities in our budget, and what things can be cut out when hard times arise?

It is of course infinitely easier to avoid difficult conversations than to lead them. But don't let this be the barrier to creating a more meaningful relationship with your partner. The risk of a few moments of discomfort should be outweighed by the potential wealth that you both could achieve, as long as there is an open, honest dialogue. Keep this vision in mind, and don't wait any longer to start the conversation.

KEY POINTS

- When it comes to making financial decisions, it's better to have a partner than an opponent. Work on your communication to ensure the former, not the latter.
- Whether you choose to separate or combine your financials, be open and honest with your partner about your habits and goals.
- Revisit the topic of money and finances regularly with your partner, especially as your respective and shared situations change.

SECRET 31

Good Health = Big Wealth

"The ultimate goal of a blessed life is physical health and mental serenity."

— Epicurus

What's the point of having massive wealth if you're physically falling apart, your friends and family don't want to be around you, or you're never present for your partner or children? These are just a few of the possible physical and mental costs of pursuing personal wealth and success.

I know them well myself because ever since I was 15 years old, I've been a workaholic.

For a number of years, I worked 3 jobs while also attending college. I wanted everything and I wanted it immediately. I earned the nickname "Old Man Will" in my mid-to-late 20's from my friends because it seemed to them that I "couldn't hang" anymore. I don't regret the way I went about my life, but I will admit that it took a toll on many of my relationships. It wasn't until my mid-30s, when I was married and my wife and I had our first child, that I started trying to balance my physical and mental workloads. I put more leverage into my life and got some of my time and space back.

So what changed for me? At the time, I was planning to work my behind off for 50 to 60 years and hopefully reap the benefits later on in retirement. I wasn't and still am not the only one who thinks that way. My life changed though when I read *The Four Hour Work Week* by Tim Ferriss. He introduced the concept of "mini retirements" to me, and from that moment, a different mindset clicked into place.

According to Ferriss, we aren't promised tomorrow, and while hard work is a good thing, we should be able to enjoy the fruits of our labor during our lives as well. We should enjoy ourselves before our bodies are too physically worn out to do so. While I don't know that most people need or want to take a 3 month sabbatical as Tim Ferriss suggests, I do believe we would benefit from instilling some balance into our hectic and ambitious lives.

I'm very passionate about my work, real estate, and helping other people, to a point where it's hard to turn it off. Your body could be physically present, but your mind continues to race with all the tasks that you want to accomplish. It can be tough to flip the switch and focus on something else equally worthwhile, but that's what's required to achieve a healthy work-life balance.

The switch becomes easier to flip when you stop and think about the fairness of the situation, as in, is it fair to your loved ones to withhold your entire focus and attention from them? You may be working hard to provide for them, but wouldn't they simply rather you take the time to engage? I have to check myself and bring myself back to the present. I remind myself why I am on this wealth building journey: to spend more time with my friends, family, and loved ones. To neglect them in the present with the hope to spend more time with them in the future doesn't make much sense. Work out a plan that offers you the flexibility to achieve your goals and enjoy what is important to you now.

The idea of creating work-life balance can be daunting, but is made easier with intentional planning. Writing down the tasks that you need to accomplish can help you get a handle on the amount of time and energy you need to earmark for each item. Below is an example of my monthly To-Do's and goals. I found this template works best for me as I figure out the things that I want do in my personal life and in my business. You can adjust this template to suit your needs, or find others that are more in style with your habits. The key to success with a list like this though is to be thoughtful and consistent. Remember that the list is a tool to help you become more efficient with your work, and isn't the end goal.

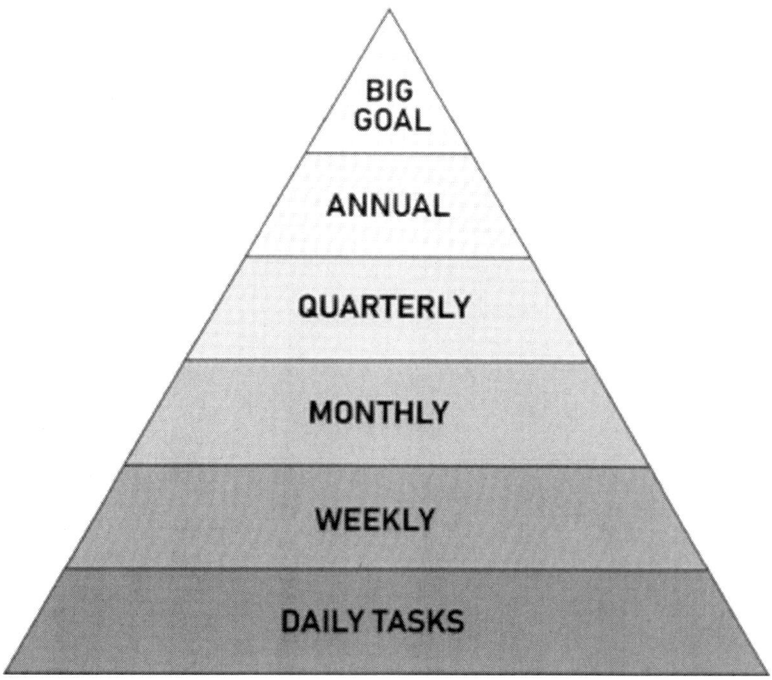

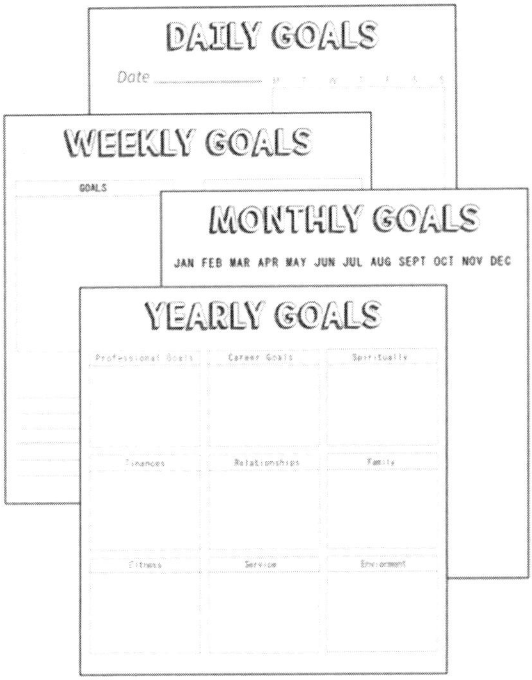

KEY POINTS

- Your mental and physical health is actually worth more than the wealth you build.
- Find time to appreciate the rewards of your hard work now and moving forward.
- Check in with yourself and make sure you are present with your friends and loved ones. You may be on this wealth-building journey for the benefit of those you love, so don't neglect them now.

SECRET 32

You Can Never Start Too Early

"Don't raise kids to have more than you had. Raise them to be more than you were."

— Anonymous

I think one of the most difficult things about my wealth building journey has been figuring out how to raise my kids once I'm financially established. Growing up, both my wife and I encountered numerous different challenges as a result of our respective socioeconomic backgrounds, and this adversity has helped us to be mentally tough. We understand how to endure hard economic times because we've lived through them before. We've always been afraid (and blessed) that that won't be the same for our kids. She and I talk on a regular basis about finding the right balance between supporting our children and letting them figure out financial responsibility on their own.

Looking back, my grandmother did really well for herself by investing in real estate. If she were still alive, she would tell you that she gave too much to her children, my father and uncle. They took her hard work and sacrifices for granted and didn't appreciate them for the gifts that they were. When my brothers and I came along, she wanted to correct the mistakes of the past. Though she did help us financially, she spent more time teaching us to fish rather than giving us fish as the saying goes. My brothers and I are stronger and more independent due to her approach with us, but I'm not even sure that this is the approach I would take with my own children.

Finding the right balance in terms of helping your children financially is up to you or you and your partner and not me and this book, but here are some thoughts for you to consider:

Set Up a Checking Account for Your Child

Both of my children have had bank profiles and savings accounts since they were 3 weeks old. When they receive birthday gifts or cash from my wife's family during Asian New Year, that money is deposited into their individual accounts. I also help them track where that money came from so they can thank that person at a later date.

The idea is for them to have their own spending cash and to help them understand the basics of savings, spending, and accounting from an early age.

Start a 529 Plan

The 529 plan is a college savings plan. The plan is funded with after-tax dollars which you can then invest into the markets. Any returns received will come out of the 529 plan tax-free, assuming that those funds are used for your child's college education.

If this is started early enough, the compounding effects of this type of savings plan can be significant. It's a proactive way to start saving money for your kids' college funds.

Help Your Kids Build Good Credit

Many credit card companies will allow you to add a minor child to your credit card profile as young as age 14 or 15. This extra 3 to 4 years of credit history prior to your son or daughter turning 18 will allow them to start off with excellent credit before they go off on their own. You can also teach them the basics of responsible credit use by providing them with a card. If you are worried about excessive charges by your child, many credit card companies will allow you to put a daily or monthly limit on the card. This prevents your child from abusing this privilege, and helps you monitor his or her spending. This is a great way to jumpstart your child's credit history and set them up for maximum leverage.

Establish a Family Trust

My wife and I put together a family trust while our children were still very young. While it seems morbid, we wanted to make sure they were protected in the event that something happened to us. The trust allows us to dictate and keep private what happens to our funds in the event that both of us die before our children reach adulthood. If either my wife or I die tomorrow, the surviving spouse will assume control of the family's assets. If we both die together, our assets are moved to the family trust. With just a will in place, our assets may be handed to minor children who will probably not have the capacity to manage those assets. With a trust, we can dictate how our funds are distributed after our deaths, along with at what age they should be disbursed to the children, and under what circumstances they should or shouldn't be distributed.

How would this work? Let's say that you pass, and your family trust holds $200,000 in assets for your children. You wouldn't want your 10-year-old to get that money immediately. Your family trust could stipulate that the money should remain liquid, so that $20,000 can be distributed immediately to the child's caretaker and be used for care and current well-being. You can also designate that another $30,000 can only be used for funding a college education. Looking ahead, $50,000 may be earmarked just for the purpose of serving as a down payment on a home. This leaves the last $100,000 that will only be distributed to your child at the age of 35, for whatever needs they see fit.

If you're interested in putting together a family trust, talk to an estate planning attorney and he or she can outline all of your options. If you aren't, consider adopting some of the other options discussed above to jumpstart your kids' finances. Start thinking about how to protect your wealth and provide for your children now before something catastrophic happens to you. Doing so will set a good example for them, and teach them financial literacy and responsibility. I hope that one day they will look upon your hard work and foresight and appreciate the gifts that you gave them, as I do for my grandmother.

KEY POINTS

- Prepare your children for a healthy relationship with money and financial responsibility.
- Open a checking account for your children, start a college savings plan, and/or help your children build good credit before they go off on their own.
- Set up a family trust to ensure your finances will be well-spent and allocated properly if something happens to you.

MONEY SMARTS

Burgers Or Real Estate?

While McDonald's Restaurants may sell hamburgers and soft drinks, the corporation is heavily involved the real estate business. McDonald's owns billions in real estate around the world.

The vast majority of McDonald's are franchises and the McDonalds corporation owns the land which they then rent to the franchisee.

McDonald's brings in billions in annual rental revenue from it's massive real estate portfolio.

MONEY SMARTS

Now is Better Than Later

If you start saving $1000 per month at the age of 20, and invest that money for an average rate of return at 6%, at the age of 60 you will have a total of $2,001,448.19

If you start saving $1000 per month at the age of 30, and invest that money for an average rate of return at 6%, at the age of 60 you will have a total of $1,009,537.62

Starting 10 Years Sooner Increased Your Savings by Close To $1,000,000

SECRET 33

Stay Humble and Stay Hungry

"No matter how hard you work, someone else is working harder."

— Elon Musk

I have friends that ask me all the time, why do I work so hard if I'm supposed to be building up my wealth passively? I'd like to think I'm doing pretty well for myself, so why do I seem to be hustling harder than most? That quality for putting in more effort to get better results is what I call hunger, and for me it stems from 2 places.

The first is fear. Here the game of Monopoly is a great example. Let's say you're doing really well, and by all accounts you seem to be winning. Now, say that you go around a couple times on the board and land on your friend's hotel at Boardwalk and then again at Park Place. How do you feel now? Just a few rolls of the dice changed things for you. Life is the same way. A major health bills. A death in the family. A disability. A fire. A car accident. Job loss. Or a virus that shuts down the global economy. These are things you can't prepare for, and while you can buy insurance or put other mechanisms in place, these events could present major financial, emotional, and mental blows to you.

Wealthy people work harder than most because they know that their circumstances can change overnight, as easily as rolling the dice. Fear is a hell of a motivator and it's okay to have a little fear push you but not consume you.

The second reason for my hunger is obsession. Whether right or wrong, it feels good to win, and it's hard to let that feeling go. Society looks at obsession as a bad word, but I think you can have healthy obsessions. I would argue that Olympic athletes are obsessed with their sports of choice. Why do we view people who want to be the fastest runners in the world or the greatest swimmers of all time as heroes, but look at someone who wants to build massive wealth as greedy or evil?

LeBron James is one of the greatest basketball players ever to play the sport. He spends $1 million per year on his physical fitness. He's already at the top of his professional game, so why doesn't he just relax? Because he's obsessed.

That's exactly the reason he continues to be at the top of the rankings. I'm obsessed with my financial well-being because I know what it feels like to live in poverty. I also understand the risk of the middle class. I understand how quickly things can change for anyone. I work hard so my family can continue to live a certain lifestyle, so my wife and I can retire in comfort, so we can take of our parents, and so my kids can understand what hard work is and to appreciate it.

KEY POINTS

- Life can change at any moment, and despite success earned today, failure can strike tomorrow.
- A little fear is natural as a motivation to keep going and continue building wealth.
- Not all obsessions are unhealthy—if you're truly passionate about your goals, obsession can be fuel for the fire.

SECRET 34

Graduation is Just the Beginning: Keep Learning

"Rich people have small TVs and big libraries, and poor people have small libraries and big TVs."

— Zig Ziglar

At first blush, the preceding quote can seem like a dig about how people choose to entertain themselves, but I assure you that is not what I am implying. I like this statement for its simplicity, and that it underscores the value of education. Financial education is maybe even the most valuable aspect, behind the fundamentals of reading and mathematics. The world is forever changing around us and we have to adapt if we want to survive. This applies to your profession as well, where you likely have to continue to perfect your skills in order to stay informed and successful in your career.

For instance, I'm in real estate. My job is not just to read books on real estate, but also those on marketing, sales, home design, and other areas that are pertinent to my specific career niche. I don't need to become a professional home stager, but I should be familiar with what's needed and what goes into the job. Moving beyond the basics, I may want to educate myself about photography, copywriting, and virtual home tours in the hopes of someday growing my brand. Of course, you and I both understand that time is limited, and every choice has a trade-off, so here are some ways that you can keep yourself in the know while maintaining efficiency:

Keep Reading

Pick a specific day and time to dedicate 30 to 60 minutes to yourself and read something new. Make it a goal to read this new content as often as you like, and don't sacrifice this time for something else. You could leave the book on your nightstand to remind yourself to read a chapter before bed. Or bring the book to work and use part of your lunch break to dive into that topic. Not a reader? Then find the audiobook version and listen to it on the train or in your car during your work commute. Most Americans haven't read a book since they left high school or college. Don't be like the majority. Carve out this time for yourself and stay consistent.

Learn from Podcasts

Podcasts are very popular now. There seems to be a Podcast on every topic imaginable. Whatever you want to learn more about, I'm sure there's a show that addresses that interest. You can even listen to Podcasts without having an iPhone, as long as you have access to the Internet. The best advantage of a Podcast is that you can listen to them for however long you like. Full episodes can be up to an hour long or as short as 10 minutes. Listen to all of the episode, or as much as you can in one sitting. And that's actually another reason why learning from Podcasts is so versatile – you don't really need to be sitting while listening. Put on a Podcast while you're preparing dinner, while you're in the shower, while you're working out, or even while you're folding laundry. Whatever it is that you do, make sure you're able to pay attention to the content, and if you can't, simply replay the episode another time when you can focus better.

Attend Tradeshows and Seminars

Whatever your industry is, there are most likely events pertaining to that field that you could find on platforms like Meetup.com or Eventbrite. Search for local gatherings to increase your opportunities in meeting new vendors and professionals in the industry. Another option includes attending mini trade shows. These usually offer breakout sessions and learning opportunities for little or no money. Be proactive and make a list of all the things that are coming to your market in the next 6 months; mark them down on your calendar and plan your schedule around them. Make it a point to get to a few and learn something new.

Search YouTube

YouTube is my go-to place for everything I want to know. Without fail, I can always find someone on YouTube willing to teach me a specific skill about which I have no clue. In the past, I've referred to YouTube to learn how to build a website, use my camera better, or advertise my business on Instagram. I also check YouTube on a regular basis for real estate, investing, and other financial matters. Just like with Podcasts, YouTube is a convenient and fast way to learn information when I am pressed for time, and is generally from people who have already done the legwork of testing their methods.

However, you decide to further your education, remember that the goal is to stay informed so that you can expand on your current situation and work towards your goals of financial freedom. Education, like everything else in life, can come at a cost, so be selective on how you spend your time and money. Overall, self-directed learning is an ongoing process that becomes its own reward when you choose to learn what interests you.

KEY POINTS

- Become a life-long scholar and ditch past-times that prevent you from growing your knowledge.
- Stay informed on the evolving nature of the real estate business and surrounding factors through reading, Podcasts, or YouTube.
- Attend a couple of networking events and seminars a year to pick up on new trends or strategies.

Secret 35

Sometimes You Can Put the Cart Before the Horse

"Buildings don't move, but neighborhoods change all the time."

— Anonymous

In Secret 27, we discussed how a property deed could show ownership without those names also appearing on the mortgage. In some instances, this can work to your advantage and allow you to become a property owner without the hassle of a full sale.

Below is an excerpt from an email that I received from a client not too long ago. It highlights an issue that some people may face with their parents or grandparents, as caring for the elders' homes becomes more difficult.

Hi Willie,

My grandmother has a 2-family home that she would like to keep in our family. My sisters and I grew up in this house, and she has asked me to buy it from her, but I'm not sure how. On top of that, the house needs a tremendous amount of work. After coming up with a down payment I would have to figure out how to get the *money to make repairs. I've done some research and know the house would be worth $400,000 after repairs, and my grandmother owes roughly $175,000 on the house today. We would need another $100,000 for repairs. My grandmother could stay in one unit rent-free and the other unit could be rented out and would cover the mortgage. I don't want to miss this opportunity, but I have very little cash for a down payment and repairs. The bank is asking me for 25% down ($44,000) as this would be my third home and an investment property.*

My response to the client was this:

Thanks for reaching out.

You should consider doing a deed transfer and a cash out refinance. (See Secret 16 for a refresher on this.) Right now, your grandmother's name is on the current mortgage and the deed. With the help of an attorney, transfer the name on your grandmother's deed (with her permission of course), so that you become the owner of the property. Once you have completed this, you now have a home with some equity. Instead of approaching the bank for a mortgage to purchase, you can now pursue a cash out refinance. Essentially, you have taken over your grandmother's mortgage, and are looking to refinance a new one. Here's what the numbers would look like if you went with this option:

-$300,000 cash out refinance & new mortgage

-$175,000 to pay off grandmother's old mortgage

-$100,000 cash in hand for needed repairs

-$25,000 closing cost, investment reserve fund

Once you are able to get the house into your name, pull out the cash you need for the renovations, put your grandmother into a better functioning home that is now fixed up, and fix up the rental unit while it covers the mortgage. You could keep the house in your family, and still have about $100,000 in equity: $400,000 value - $300,000 in debt.

There are 2 caveats to be aware of in this scenario. First, you want to make sure you understand your gift tax laws for the local area.

When your grandmother signs the deed over to you, she essentially gifts you the equity within the property. Talk to your attorney and local CPA about any tax potential ramifications for you and your grandmother.

You should also be familiar with the *due-on-sale clause* in most mortgages. Most mortgage companies have this clause within their contracts. When your grandmother transfers the mortgage out of her name into your name, it technically counts as a sale. The clause states that the mortgage balance is now due in full.

In my experience, very few banks act on this clause, and in this scenario, we would only be carrying grandma's mortgage for a short period of time. As long as your grandma is still making the mortgage payments, it's unlikely the bank will act on this clause. You should consult legal counsel and make sure you're familiar with local laws before putting something like this in place.

KEY POINTS

- If acquiring a home from a loved one, look into a deed transfer and cash-out refinance option.
- You can do repairs on a property using equity from the home itself instead of through a new mortgage.
- Consult with lawyers in your local area regarding laws regarding gift-taxes and due-on-sale clauses contained in mortgages.

Final Thoughts:

Dear friend, I am so honored that you have finally made it to the end of my book. I hope that you found within these pages some insight into the world of wealth-building through real estate investing. Thank you for choosing to spend your time learning about this topic that is still so fascinating to me by picking up this book. I want you to understand that I am truly passionate about this career path, but my road to success wasn't evenly paved. My intention was to give you a glimpse of something bigger than even my ambitions, and to inspire you to want a piece of it for yourself. I wrote this book to offer you advice about how to get started on realizing your own dreams of success, advice which is based off of hard-earned experience. I wouldn't want for you to make the same mistakes that I did, and so I developed each "secret" with a specific lesson in mind that I essentially learned the hard way.

I also wrote this book in the hopes of welcoming you to a growing network of like-minded individuals who seek support and knowledge for financial freedom. Consider yourself a member of Wealth Builder Nation now. I hope you use the information that you have learned here to reach out to others and at last reach your full earning potential.

Finally, I want you to envision a life where you can have it all: family, friends, health, and wealth. Use this image as motivation to work hard! Wherever you are on your wealth-building journey, always remember where you started from, where you want to go, and the people and tools that can help get you there.

Sincerely,

Willie J. Mandrell III

Bonus Secrets

Bonus Secret A

Never Buy a Car on Monthly Payment

"Always focus on the front windshield and not the rear-view mirror."

— Colin Powell

Why is there a section in this book on buying automobiles? Because the average person owns roughly 10 vehicles during his or her lifetime. This is a total of 10 opportunities to lose money if you don't know what you're doing in the dealership. This is less of a wealth building tactic than it is a *wealth preservation* strategy. Allow me to give you an insider peek at how to keep your hard-earned money in your pocket, based on my experiences in car sales.

There are 3 ways car dealers try to make money off of buyers. Keep these in mind for the next time you need to buy a new vehicle, and want to maintain the upper hand.

One: The Sale of the Car

Car dealers make money on the sales of cars. Auto dealers typically buy cars at 1 price, whether new or used, and attempt to sell it to you at a different price for a profit.

First off, never buy a car on monthly payment. Buy a car a car at "total price."

Here's the wrong way to do it: Car dealers will ask "what would you like to pay monthly?" You say, "$400 a month is my max," believing you're holding the line. They do the math and present you with a car that's $425 a month. If you're savvy, you hold the line at $400. The salesperson will go back to the manager's office, acting as if this is a real struggle they're fighting for you. They come back out and say, "let's move forward at $400 a month." What you don't know is you could have gotten the car for $375 per month if you bought it on price instead of in payments.

The best way to buy is to have your math and pre-approval already done prior to entering the dealership. Let's say the car you want has a sticker price of $23,500. Using a loan calculator on Google (assuming an interest rate of 3%), I can see that my payment will be $425 per month over a 60 month term. In the above example, the car dealer essentially offered me the car at sticker price initially. Assuming you pushed back a little on the monthly payment and held the line, and they reduced the monthly price to get me to my $400. You've felt like you've won bu in reality you may not have won at all. If you focused on price instead of payment you could have negotiated $2500 off the sticker price. This 2500$ reduction would have brought you monthly payment down to 375$, which is below the 400$ you initially asked for.

Two: The Up-Sell

After you discover the car and have fallen in love, the dealer will now attempt to sell you floor mats, the sound system upgrade, leather seats, or whatever the latest electronics package may be.

This one's easy. Just be prepared for the up-sell. Find the things that you want online and do your research prior to getting into the dealership. Many times, the dealership has such a high mark-up that it's easier and less expensive to buy these things aftermarket.

Know what you want prior to going to the dealership and don't make emotional decisions on the spot.

Three: The Financing

The auto dealer will offer you financing after you've negotiated the price of your car. They are also making money by lending you the money to buy this vehicle. For example, "Honda Financial Services" is the lending arm for the Honda brand.

1-2-3. This is how most people operate when it comes to purchasing a new car, when in reality, it should be 3-2-1. Ideally you would find your financing prior to entering the dealership. Where could you look for this though? You can talk to your local credit union which is probably where you will find the best rates. You can ask for a car pre-approval and then run some examples on what your payment will be based on different purchase prices. This allows you to go into a dealership knowing what your maximum purchase price is versus negotiating on a monthly payment.

When I walk into a dealership, I have a letter from my bank in hand and my financing in place. I'm prepared to turn down all unnecessary up-sells and keep my emotions in check. I know that my maximum purchase price is $22,000 based on my conversations and calculations I've done prior to going in. I now just have a single objective: to get the total sales price down as low as I possibly can.

If you're going to lease a vehicle, buy on payment. I know what you're thinking: we just talked about not buying on payment. Well, leasing is the only time you're going to be buying based on payment, because you're not buying the vehicle outright.

Before you lease based on payment, though, determine whether leasing is the right option for you. For instance, you always want to watch out for mileage restrictions and make sure you're leasing a car that fits your lifestyle.

Bottom line, the more prepared you are for the song and dance of the auto dealer, the better deal you will walk away from the dealership with.

KEY POINTS

- Never buy a car based on monthly payment value, purchase based on total price.
- Prepare yourself for the up-sell and do your research on desired features before entering the dealership.
- Avoid dealership financing options, and arrive with a pre-approval from your trusted local lender.

BONUS SECRET B

Become Your Own Captain of Industry

"Good things happen to those who hustle."

— Anais Nin

Take some time to seriously think about the wealthiest people in the world. How did they achieve success? I think you'll find that most either started a business, invested in somebody else's business, invested in the market, or invested in real estate.

Investing in someone else's business and investing in the stock market takes the control out of your hands and puts your retirement and financial freedom on somebody else to secure. I'm not saying that you shouldn't take either of these 2 approaches, just that you shouldn't rely on them solely for your financial security.

It is my personal belief that everyone should own their own company. The company does not need to be the next Amazon, nor do you need to leave your day job to start and run that company. Now more than ever it's easy find something you're good at or enjoy doing *and* make money from it. You should always be looking at creating additional streams of income for yourself and family. Relying on your day job as your only source of income is borderline foolish. Automation and computers are taking over and will continue to take over many industries. Even if you feel your job is protected from automation, a bad economic climate and industry downturns could put a dent in your salary or even eliminate your job.

Your additional business or side hustle doesn't need to immediately replace your income. The idea is to supplement your primary income with the option of replacing it in the future. If you make $50,000 today from your job, having a side hustle that'll produce you an additional $10,000 a year is huge.

When considering what to do for additional streams of income, find something that doesn't seem like more work for you. Ask yourself, what do you enjoy doing? What are you really good at that you're going to offer the public? What is your spouse really good at and what do they enjoy doing? How can you take this skill and bring it online? What can you do in your spare time as to not trade additional time for money? How can you use what you already know well to make additional streams of income?

The following are some options to help identify your side hustle, and how to get after it:

Upwork.com - maybe you can help people virtually in your spare time with marketing, resume writing, Web design, SEO, video editing, or thousands of other things.

teachable.com - Do you have a skill set that you can record and offer classes online in? Even if you don't feel comfortable in front of the camera, you can just record yourself speaking while doing a computer screen capture. Check out my profile to get some ideas of how you can set your recording up.

Fiverr.com - Another service where you can offer your skill set online to create an additional revenue stream.

One of the greatest books I've read on side hustles and additional streams of income was *The Four Hour Work Week* by Tim Ferriss.

KEY POINTS

- Investing in the markets or someone else's business is risky.
- Instead, find a way to invest in yourself by creating a side job that can supplement your income and help build security for the future.
- Explore your interests and find the best place to offer your services, as with the Internet, there are plenty of new options available.

Randoms Answers to Questions I've Been Asked

Can You Tell Us More About Why/How You Bought Your In-Laws House from Them?

When my wife got pregnant, we started looking at the cost of daycare. This was something we had never done before, so we weren't familiar with the cost and how expensive it could be. We found that most of the daycare centers that we were interested in charged just about $100 a day for full-time care, or close to $2000 each month.

I remember telling my wife that $2000 a month is crazy. "That's a mortgage payment!" She agreed and said that her parents' mortgage payment was almost the exact same amount. We realized that we'd rather pay the $2000 a month to her parents every month, basically making their mortgage payments ourselves.

We talked to her mother about retiring from her job and staying home with her new grandchild. She agreed, and by the time my daughter was born, we had the best situation possible. A couple years later, my son was born, and the savings multiplied.

My in-laws actually put the deed to the house in our name as well, similar to what was described in Bonus Secret ##. In this way, my wife and I received all the tax benefits that came with paying for and operating the house. We now have an additional asset in our portfolio that's appreciating value, and each month the debt is being reduced, creating equity and building further wealth.

Can You Purchase A 2nd Home For Yourself With A Low Down Payment Loan?

Often you can find mortgage programs that allow you to buy a second home with as little as 5% out of pocket. This is especially important if you have aging parents that need somewhere to live. The mortgage company may ask you to provide proof that your parents can't afford the mortgage themselves, and if so, will often allow you to buy the property for them. This is a great way to put an additional asset into your portfolio. You'll also know that the property is being taken care of by people whom you love and trust. If the home for your parents happens to be a multi-family, you may be able to allow them to live for less than what they would have been paying in rent if the additional units can cover the majority of your costs.

Does It Make Sense for Me to Buy Rental Property In The Area Where My Kids Go to College?

As a realtor, I have sold many homes to investors who bought property for their children to live in. Instead of paying thousands per semester in boarding fees for a college dorm room while receiving nothing in return, they opted to buy a rental near the university for their child. Some of the investors even took it a step further and had their kid rent out the additional rooms in the house to other students at the university. So not only was their kid living rent-free, but the mortgage was also being paid for by other students. I had one investor who had 2 kids going to the same university but a few years apart. This was a great strategy for him for a total of 7 years and worked out so well that he decided to keep the house as a college rental.

What are Your Thoughts On Vacation Home & Using Them As A Rental?

Vacation homes can be great as well. If you have a destination that you frequent, it may make sense to buy another residence there. If a second home doesn't seem feasible, there are also mortgage programs that allow for the purchase of a vacation home with as little as 10% down.

Many investors buy vacation homes for places they travel to often. They have the luxury of not having to stay in a hotel or share amenities with other guests. With the rise in popularity of sites like Airbnb or VRBO, you can rent the space out and earn additional income when you're not using it.

What Are SBA Loans & How Can I Use Them To My Advantage?

SBA loans allow you to buy business property with as little as 10% down. If your business operates using more than 51% of the space, it should qualify for SBA lending. If you need office space to run your property management business, you could look at the option of purchasing space instead of renting. This is an amazing program that allows small business owners a chance to get into another asset with very little funds out-of-pocket. Instead of paying another landlord for space and having very little control, consider using an SBA loan to break into commercial real estate. The deal can be sweetened if you purchase commercial space with multiple units.

Similar to the residential side, you can now have a commercial tenant covering a chunk of your cost every month. You can find out more about SBA loans at SBA.gov. You will want to speak to a local commercial real estate lender, as they would need to partner with the SBA to offer the loan to you.

What is "Lifestyle Inflation" and How Does It Affect Me?

It's called lifestyle inflation or lifestyle creep. I've heard it called multiple things, but it's a very real phenomenon. As people make more money, they tend to spend more money, as things that weren't necessities before become necessities when additional cash comes into the equation. It's very hard to control, but absolutely necessary if you are to accumulate wealth.

I found the best way to avoid lifestyle creep is just to keep on top of your budget. Make sure you have a budget, it's reviewed regularly, and it's very hard for new items to make it onto the budget. Most people have trouble with lifestyle inflation because they don't have a budget in place. They don't know where their money is going and everything seems important. Money tends to burn a hole in your pocket, and when you have it, you try to find reasons to get rid of it.

The other thing you must do is track your spending. That's where your financial management software is going to come in handy. Treat your life like a business. A good businessperson knows all of his income and, more importantly, all of his expenses. If you're tracking the money going out, you can figure out whether or not you stayed on budget each month or how things went awry. You also have to get your entire household onboard. If you're catching rainwater with 1 bucket while your spouse is punching additional holes in the roof, no one stays dry.

Have You Ever Used A Lease Option to Take Control of Property?

A lease option is a very cool way to take control of the property if you don't yet have the money or you're not entirely sure you want to purchase the property. A few years into starting my brokerage business, I found the perfect office space up for sale. My business was still relatively new and I didn't want to commit to a down payment just then, but I also didn't want to lose the opportunity. There was very little commercial inventory in this area of the city, and I knew if I didn't act on it, I may not be able to find something similar.

I knew the seller wanted to sell, but I felt like his market price was a little high. I decided to offer him a 12-month lease. Included in the lease, I had the option to buy the property for his full asking price during the next 12 months. The seller would win because he filled up an empty space and I was now covering his monthly cost. I won because I got control of the space with very little money out of my pocket, and it also secured a future purchase price for myself. I was essentially able to test out the space without having to commit to the purchase. The seller also was able to secure a potential selling price that was slightly above market. It was a win-win for us both. Sometimes winning in real estate is about finding a way to take control of an asset and then figuring out what to do later on.

Lease options are complex, and you do have to be careful on the commercial side. In residential real estate there are many state and local laws that help protect tenants. Many of the contracts are standard in form. On the commercial side, this is not the case. There are templates you can use. but for the most part, all the language needs to be negotiated by both parties. You shouldn't look at this as an obstacle, though. It's actually an opportunity, since now almost everything is up for negotiation. Find a deal that works for you.

When Buying Property, Are You Always Looking for The Lowest Price?

The inexperienced real estate investor thinks everything is centered around price: lower price good and higher price bad. For the most part, this is true, but you're missing a whole host of opportunities if this is the extent of your thinking. Real estate can be about terms just as much as it is about price.

What are terms? Terms are all the other elements up for negotiation. For instance, the deposit amount, the closing date, items left at the property, tenant vacancies, contingencies, and a host of smaller items that can be negotiated. Let's review a few of these:

Let's say I just made a big purchase that took up a good chunk of my cash, and a few days later, another great home-run deal hits my desk. Do I throw my hands up and say I can't do it because I don't have the cash? Do I let a home-run deal slide away? The answer is no - I focus instead on the terms of the deal.

Maybe I give the seller the full asking amount and offer a smaller-than-usual deposit to hold the property. If the seller is focused on getting her price, maybe I also offer an extended closing date, allowing me more time to gather funds or find a partner with funding. Or I make the deal contract contingent upon the building being delivered vacant and free of tenants. I do this because I know it would take an extended period of time for the tenants to find new housing or for the landlord to take them through eviction court. I can use this time to get the additional funds that I need to make the purchase. I've completed hundreds of real estate transactions as a buyer, seller, or broker, and not 1 of them has been identical. The big takeaway would be to understand that you have more in your tool bag to work with than just price. You can often win by negotiating hard on the terms of the deal.

How Do I Know When It's Time to Delegate or Hire Help to Grow My Business?

In the beginning of your career, time is your biggest asset. You have more time than you have money. As your real estate portfolio grows, that balance shifts in the opposite direction. Your schedule fills up, and you end up with more money than time. Understanding that shift is important.

In the beginning, you try to do everything yourself. You take on projects and assignments you're not good at, but you have the time to figure it out. As you have some success, you'll have to learn to use leverage. It can be a real struggle giving up control. There's an age-old saying that state, "If you want something done right you have to do it yourself." This doesn't always work in business.

Part of growth is giving up complete control and allowing others to assist in your success. Remember that the "others" can be people, systems, tools, money—anything that makes your life more automated and simplified.

When you have more time, use it to make money. When you have more money than time, use that money to buy back some of your time. Leverage is the key to business growth.

ABOUT THE AUTHOR

Willie J. Mandrell is a self-made multi-millionaire real estate investor, broker, coach, lecturer & author. As a buyer, seller, and broker, he's been involved with over $200 million in real estate transactions. He has been featured in numerous trade magazines and he is a frequent guest on real estate and wealth-related podcast, television, & radios shows across the US. Willie is also a member of the Forbes Real Estate Council.